Crisis

By
Ai Carlo

ISBN: 978-1-0688170-1-4

Prologue

Once upon a time, Toronto, Ontario, was known for its diversity, its nature, being a lot of parents' second home and the first home to their children. Everybody from all across the world would aspire to start a new life for their families here. They would come here looking for refuge, and would be able to live a prosperous and positive life. In modern days, Toronto has turned into the place that most people are being forced to get away from.

The income needed to get a mortgage on a home in Toronto is $250,000. The top one percent of Canadians make an average $201,000 a year. This means at the time that I am writing this, the top one percent of Canadians can't afford a home in Toronto. The blatant, mass gentrification the city has been under for the past decade has created a massive increase in the number of individuals and families facing and navigating homelessness. One thing to know about Torontonians, they have an extraordinarily strong heart. Even with this crushing poverty, most refuse to leave. We keep our heads high and force ourselves to find a way to make things work. The ones who stick around have a choice to make everyday, and as much as they try to do good, the only way to handle their business is to be drawn into evil surroundings.

The city of Scarborough amalgamated into the rest of the city of Toronto in the late nineteen-ninety's. Scarborough is now the largest and easternmost borough in the City of Toronto. A longtime destination for immigrants starting their lives in Canada, Scarborough has been home to many success stories. Unfortunately, the borough is more famous for the negativity attached to its name. A lot of the critiques of Scarborough come from the outside looking in instead of considering life on the inside. The horrors and trauma survived by the people of Scarborough have not received the appropriate humanizing attention for remediation. The goal of this book is to shed light and humanity onto those survivors.

The story of Daniel Ibanez is one of thousands in the city of Toronto. A young male, with big dreams coming from an impoverished broken home, whose only desire is to save himself, his family, and his community. Every single person who grew up in a city like Toronto knows someone like Daniel. Failure is not an option, no matter what is thrown his way, he needs to get back up and keep fighting for his future. Take these words home and think them through.

Currently, on any given night in Toronto, there are over nine thousand people experiencing homelessness. In one of the coldest countries on the planet, in what was promised to people as a place to escape, one person homeless should be considered one too many. Each and every single one of these people have a story, have dignity, and need and deserve somewhere to live. A significant percentage of these people are youth and young adults coming from extremely vulnerable situations. This book is about one of them.

Table of Contents

Chapter One:
Summertime Sadness

It is the end of the summer. We were by the water one last time, it was our favorite place. It held so many different memories. Our first time skipping rocks, our first time learning about each other's lives and what we've been through, our first time holding hands, all the young love milestones up to our first kiss. Today might be our last kiss, and if it is we are going to make it count. *Real love is releasable; if two souls are meant to find each other, they will, and no matter how far apart they may seem, they will always reconnect in the end.*

Mimi broke the silence, "Can I ask you something?", "You already know you can ask me anything," I said quietly. "How often are we going to talk once I get there?" I touched her hand, interlaced my fingers with hers, and looked deep in her eyes and said, "Every day. Nothing changes between us. I don't not know when I'm going to see you again, but you can message me every day and I am going to answer every day." I lifted my arms and reached in for a hug, and then a kiss.

The sun was starting to rise, so I walked Mimi back to her house. I saw her dad outside helping her mom pack up. She didn't want us to get caught so she gave me one last hug and I told her to message me when she touched down in Florida. I turned around to head back some since I live a couple blocks away.

I met Mimi in the seventh grade; We were about to enter tenth. As soon as I met her I knew I was going to marry her one day. She had beautiful brown skin, thick jet black hair, a smile to die for, and somehow her spirit that outshines all of that. The second we met there was an energy like we knew each other from a past life. She will always be my first example of real love, if nothing else, and I had to be ready.

Mimi's mom got a job all the way in Orlando, Florida. Unfortunately, there was no possible way for Mimi to stay and finish out high school here, and I had just spent most of my last summer with her in summer school. My biggest regret will always be that I should have made more time for her while I could. We've been together for three years, everyone keeps saying I'm young and it will be easy to move on to someone else.. I have a different focus in mind going into this next year of life.

My name's Daniel but everybody calls me Crisis. It's been my nickname for as long as I can remember, and for the past year, it has been my stage name. Icome from a musical family on both sides. Both my mother and father were singers, every type of music you can think of: Hip hop, R&B, rock, reggae, calypso, disco, oldies, everything was always playing in my house growing up, so I was hip various eras and genres from a very young age

Unfortunately, neither of my parents saw any type of success. There was never any type of success story or let alone support in their time to be able to have had that break in Toronto. Then life got a bit more complicated. My father has been locked up since my early childhood and my mother was deemed unfit to care for me and my siblings. My Aunt Lala ended up taking us in, she wanted to be a poet and always encouraged me to write.

Territory divided people where we lived, everything east of the main intersection belonged to the Crips, everything west

2

belonged to the Bloods. Our neighborhood was like a family, east and west side kids were close like cousins in elementary school, attending the same programs and hanging out. By high school, the cousin becomes more like a distant relative you. I got my start in the street life a little earlier than most. I've had a close connection with the Crips through my older sister Natasha and my cousin Jay since the age of ten.

Jay was the eldest of the kids in the house, Natasha was closer in age to me and used to be my favorite. We would always be like best friends until the time I started getting around the same lifestyle as her and Jay. She thought something was off about Jay and his friends bringing me around so early on, I just didn't see it yet.

I've always looked up to Jay, he's the main reason I got into music and the neighbourhood. Everything I did was following in his footsteps. Jay had me jump off the porch at 10 years old, brought me along with his people to every function, and we were always making moves in the streets. Even though I was younger than everyone, I always felt like I belonged when I was with Jay and (the boys, his friends, whichever term).

Natasha's dream was to open a beauty salon and barber shop. She wanted to get into an industry that had consistent business and people will always need haircuts. She hustled to get it started and was hoping by some point next year, she would be open for business. Jay on the other hand loved the lifestyle so much he just wanted to stay making money from the streets forever. It He never landed him in any serious trouble so there was no real never any motivation to leave it alone.

Natasha would only let me go outside if I went twice as hard promoting my music. She had a rule that I was to never glorify street life in my music. I had no intentions of doing that. I just wanted to be a teenager, it costs money to go to the movies, go out to eat, and make music. Most of my content was about having the best bars, a couple of songs for Mimi, and clothes and jewelry. Teenager type of music.

I had a big following on social media. I would always perform at any event around the city that would let me in despite my age. Talent shows at other high schools, all ages open mic events, anything that I could get myself involved in, I would make it happen. I start each day with checking my messages on every platform. Today I got a very unexpected message. from a record executive at an independent label and management company.

Hello Crisis,

I am an A&R from Digital Records and after a full review of your catalgue. I would like to offer you a distribution deal for your first project. We have worked with several other Hip-Hop acts and feel your image and sound fits our brand. We are based in Los Angeles, CA which would require travelling on your end. Based on the age listed in your artist biography, we would need to have your parent/guardian's signature to start the process.

Please let us know at your earliest convenience if you are ready to take the next steps in your career and allow us to take your music to a professional level.

Best Regards,

Michael Williams, A&R

Digital Records

I felt a rush of emotions. I was excited, I was in disbelief, I was nervous, This could be the moment I've been waiting for my whole life. It could also be someone trying to play a joke or set me up, worse, someone scamming for money. Whatever it was, I knew I had to keep it to myself for the time being. Imagine I went and told everybody about this and it didn't happen, nobody would ever let me live it down.

I would spend my time at the youth centre or by the mall when I wasn't in the neighbourhood with the family. It was usually the safest place to be aside from the Bluffs, and it was where my best friends Devon and Taylor would be. I met when I was young at the youth centre. When we met up we'd play basketball, run on the track, and sometimes played tag in the weight room (but I didn't tell you that). Either way, they were down for me, and I was down for them.

Devon was just as ambitious as I was, if not more. He's dreamt of playing in the NBA since we were little. He was a starting point guard at our high school and was potentially moving up to shooting guard for the next school year. We would always be at each other's houses, his family was nice and welcoming.We always kept each other accountable to reach our goals and never felt like we were competing, we were al just two kids with big dreams.

Taylor on the other hand was more conventional. Both his parents met in college and work in finance. He just wanted to follow them in their footsteps and enjoy life in the meantime. All three of us tried for straight A's in school, but Taylor was the one who actually got all A's in every class. We had no idea how he did it. Either way, these were the friends who knew how to keep me one foot out of my family's business, and encouraged me to stay focused on the big picture in life.

The plan for today was the usual, head to the gym to meet Taylor and Devon, run a game of ball, watch a movie, then head to the mall. I got on the bus outside my complex, paid my fare, and then looked for a seat. I saw Devon at the back with his ball in his hands and his duffle bag taking up the seat beside him.

"What you saying broski?" Devon said. "Bout to make you start coming off the bench in a month" I replied, we both started laughing. "You hear from Tay yet?" I continued. "His dad dropped him at the mall already, he'll meetup at the station."

"What you think he's doing to pass the time?" I asked. "You know exactly what he's doing" Devon replied.

Tay tended to tell every girl he met that he was best friends with me and Devon to try to impress her. He would usually do this in front of us to try to hype us up, but he would also just love the respect and clout he would get from us. Anyone else would get cut off, but Tay got a pass because he was really day one, He earned it. one thing you always must do, no matter what, is stay loyal to the people who believed in you when no one else did.

We got to the bus station and saw Tay making out with a girl by the bus stop as soon as we got off. We walked up to them, he lifted his head up and said "SEE?? I told you!" We both just laughed, gave him daps, and said what up to the girl. "Her name is Tiffany. Don't be shy, guys!" We shook Tiffany's hand and she gave him one last hug before getting on her bus. "I'll call you!!" Tay shouted. Right after the bus door closed, Tay turned back to us and said, "you guys know I'm not really going to call her, right?" Me and Devon just locked eyes and said in our heads knew exactly what he was going to be doing.

"You see Mimi yet, Crisis?" Tay asked as we walked up the escalator; "She didn't leave yet, right?" "Yeah man, I was with her this morning" I replied. "THIS MORNING! Did you see her last night too?" Tay started laughing and going off "Thank God her dad didn't find you, he would've moved her even farther away!" We've all been there, with the first love you experienced comes the first real heartbreak, and one friends is too immature to consider anything other than sex.

"Man, chill with all of that." I told Tay. "It wasn't even like that, it was pretty much just a date--" Tay cut me off, "Look, bro, you can go on dates with any girl in town if you want to now, you know that right? Meem's was cool, I liked her for you, bro, but she's gone. She's going to be in Florida, and you know what they got in Florida? She's going to find a nice celebrity, he's going to be her prom date at an alligator farm or a shooting range or some shit, then they're going to be together forever!! It has been *5 hours*, it is time to move on, bro!"

Part of me wanted to laugh with my homies, another part of me felt like he was right. She is going to move on and find better, we might not reconnect at the end of the story, maybe our souls were just meant to introduce each other to love. Whether Tay was right or wrong, I had to be ready for either reality.

Tay sees a pretty girl outside of a Footlocker while we're walking around the mall. She had, glasses, full lips, curly hair, and wore a grey dress. She looked annoyed, she certainly wasn't in the mood for whatever antics Tay had in mind. He poked me then pointed right at her, "You know you could get that girl's number right?" "Fam, can you let me wait til Mimi gets to the airport first? With your Poindexter ass" I looked back at him and chuckled. "Whatever man, if you're not going to, I will."

Tay leaves me and Devon to go after the girl. She was waiting in line for bubble tea at a store closeby. His first move was to wait in line, she picked up her order and sat down. Next, we saw Tay scurry out of line to get to her table, "I SAID NO, BOZO" she shouted, gesturing for him to go away.

"Nobody needs a girl who acts like that anyway." Tay huffed as he ran back up to us. "Yeah, it's time to go to the court you wilding out" Devon told him. "Hey, don't hate me because I believe in myself, y'all the ones who can only have one girl at a time, you can't even get a car yet and y'all want to be married. Not every girl is going to say yes, in fact, I'm more mature for respecting her right to say no." We all just started laughing as we were walking, "there's always next time" Tay winked at me.

We get to the gym and go straight to the court. We just have to change our shoes since it's still summer, we have ball shorts underneath our jeans. A few older members are there already playing a game, the good thing about a community center is it was *about community*. Everybody knows everybody, and everybody looks out for each other. It was like the block to me, only in a positive way, the perfect example of a home away from home.

The older heads gave us first ball. They passed to Devon, they check it in, and the game was on. I run to the wing, and Tay runs right under the net, all three of us are covered, Devon can't pass to me or Tay. Devon takes a step back, spins, and gets the ball to me.

I run the ball to the other wing to get away from the guy guarding me, I shoot -- it lands. 1-0, us. They pass to Devon, he goes in for the layup. The ball rolls around the rim and goes in. 2-0, us. They chuck the ball to Devon and start crowding him, leaving me and Tay wide open. Devon tries to bounce-pass me the ball, but it gets stolen in the process. Our opponent drives the ball to the net and slam dunks over Tay and me, bringing the score to 2-1. It's their ball now, Devon passes them the ball, they spread out and we each try to stay on our man.

I've always been on the shorter side, which is why I pursued music over sports. One thing I mastered in almost every sport was stealing the ball. Whether it was basketball, soccer, or football, that's where I would stand out in a game. They try an overhead pass, I jump up and take the ball in midair, drive it right to the net and try to score off the backboard. It misses, Devon grabs it off the rebound and passes it out to Tay to clear it. Tay goes for the shot from behind the line, it hits. 4-1, us. All we need is one more point to win.

The other team passes to Devon first, Devon passes it back, and then they pass the ball to me and run up to me. I see Devon guarded up, waiting for an opening, Tay's guarded too. I had about ten seconds left to make a move, I took a risk and tried to get around the guy guarding me. I made it to the three-point line when I could feel Devon running behind me. I pass the ball behind me and Devon grabs it, runs it to the net and gets a dunk for the win.

"Good game" Devon reaches out to the other team and shakes their hands, then we all shake hands and just keep shooting the ball around for a little bit. Devon's only sixteen but he already put in the 10,000 hours to master his craft before I met him. His entire life *is* basketball, and he made sure he would be the one in a million who could make it to the NBA, because he made sure he would be.

Devon and Tay are opposites; Devons an Aquarius, and Tays a Leo. Devon is focused, creative, and is someone who will not waver from whatever it is he is after, but to do that stays to himself to block out any outside noise to keep himself in the mentality he needs to be in. Tay is just super confident and loves putting himself out there no matter what manner it is and just wants to be outside all the time and be the life of the party. I am a Cancer, and I can sense a little bit of both; I always knew when to stay in my shell and when to come out and let my ideas flourish. That is why the click worked.

We checked our phones, it was 5:57pm, we knew we had to start heading home, but not yet. We started to walk back to the mall hoping to see a movie before catching the bus home. We see blue and red lights flashing through the windows as we're leaving the gym. The whole mall was blocked off, we were only inside for an hour or two, but that is how fast everything can change. A police officer starts putting the yellow numbers on the ground, someone got shot in the parking lot.

We go the other way and walk back to the bus station, pay our fare and go to the terminal to check our bus times. Tay's bus comes in minutes, mine and Devon's comes in six. "You guys want to go back tomorrow?" Tay was completely unfazed with whatever just happened at the mall. "Why man, so we can be next?" Devon responded to Tay before I interjected, "We lived in Scarborough before that happened man, you can't let stuff like that bother you. Got to just accept it exists in this world and avoid it."

Tay shook his head,; "You know you're the main one who needs to worry about this stuff, right?" I got defensive, "What are you talking about?" Tay looked at me, "Look, you're our boy for life but think about what's been going on with you lately. Your family's always been around this, and you're coming up to the age where you'll be around this kind of stuff, if you're not already. They might tell you they want you to do music, but if they needed you to ride out for them you think they wouldn't make you?" I never thought about that before. "God forbid, but what happens if you go home right now and somehow, someway your cousin's people were involved? Me and Dev are just teenagers with no ties to anybody, we are not involved in any of these gangs. *You* are the one who needs to be careful."

Tay daps me and Devon then heads onto his bus, then we walk to our terminal. "He's still mad that girl dissed him, and movies is for Tuesdays. What are we going to pay double for tomorrow?" I said to Devon. "Yeah, he didn't need to go there, but still in those situations anybody can get hit, even if it's by accident. We've seen that happen countless times." Devon said before adding, "Look, bro, I don't want you to get yourself into anything you can't get yourself out of, you know?" That was the moment I couldn't hold it in anymore. I pulled out my phone and showed Devon the e-mail from Digital.

I watch Devons face as he's holding my phone, his mouth opens wider than he can cover with his hand. He looks at me proudly, "Fam, this is you??!! You're so close to everything you've been working towards. Tell your aunt when you get home, man. You got the ticket to get away from all of this. This is what your whole family's been working for. We are going to party and celebrate tomorrow." He gave me a dap as I was coming to my stop on the bus, I got off and headed home.

Devon and Tay gave me a lot to think about today. Tay was being rude for no reason, but he was right. The longer I stay in all this, the more likely I will wind up in a situation like what happened at the mall. All I have to do is get my aunt to sign the record deal, and why wouldn't she? This was the start of a positive shift.

As soon as I walked through the door the police were inside the house arresting Jay. *The shooting at the mall was him.* The police were able to detect his cell phone in the range of a cell tower which put his location to exactly where the shots were fired at the moment they dropped. My aunt was crying, repeatedly saying "no" trying to pull the police off him. The police put handcuffs on Jay and escorted him to the car.

This turned out to be the worst possible time to ask Aunt (whatever her name is) about anything, so instead I tried to comfort her. I reached in to hug her and she rejected it, instead she went to the liquor cabinet. "Nothing but Jay coming home is going to make me feel better. They had no right to take him," she said as she was opening her rum bottle. I decided to go to my room and settle in for the night. When I plugged my phone in, I saw a notification from Mimi.

Mimi Singh *(8:06pm)*

Hey Daniel, just letting you know we got here safely, I just got into my new room!

Me *(10:08pm)*

That's good I am glad you got there ok, how was the flight?

Mimi Singh *(10:09pm)*

The flight was ok, still in shock, didn't really want to be here but I got to make the best of it right?

Me *(10:11pm)*

I feel you, it will be alright though. Just take it one day at a time and give it a chance, okay?

Mimi Singh *(10:12pm)*

I will try. No promises though.

Me *(10:13pm)*

You're starting school next week?

Mimi Singh *(10:14pm)*

Tomorrow. They start earlier here.

Me *(10:15pm)*

Oh man, let me know how it goes ok? We both had a rough day today and should try to get some sleep. Goodnight, babe!

Mimi Singh *(10:16pm)*

No don't do that, what happened?? Are you okay?

Me *(10:17pm)*

I got some sad news and might have some good news. Jay got arrested today, but I might have an opportunity with music. It is still too early to know if the opportunity is for real though.

Mimi Singh *(10:20pm)*

Oh, wow what did he do now? And believe that it's real, believe that you have put in all the work you could put in, you are doing music for the right reasons, and you deserve to be successful at it. Also, you never said ily after goodnight!

Me *(10:22pm)*

They're saying he shot somebody I don't know, my life's crazy, but I love you and I am grateful I got you in it to keep me sane.

Mimi Singh *(10:23pm)*

I love you too Daniel, and I am always going to be right here beside you, as long as you are always beside me. No matter what, I am always on your team, okay? Goodnight, babe sweet dreams and take care.

Me *(10:24pm)*

Goodnight, babe you too.

I set my alarms and settled into bed, I felt like I had to cheer up my aunt with the good news in the morning. I'm really glad I heard from Mimi, she knows how to ground me. Hearing from her would always put me at ease no matter the situation. She always was my support system. She was right, I worked hard and stayed true to myself on the journey to get this opportunity. More than anything else, it was going to be a way better path than what I see for my future through Jay.

I woke up around 7 or 8, everybody was still asleep so I walked to the store to kill time. When I got to the store I immediately looked at the TV, they usually had the news on. The report said that the victim of yesterdays mall shooting passed away and they had Jay and two other suspects in custody for the murder. My heart sank to my stomach when I read that. Jay was really going to be gone for a long time, and there wasn'thing any of us could do. All I can think about is Natasha telling me not to hang out with him and his friends, and now, how right she was.

Aunt Lala was awake when I got back, but she still seemed upset. She was drunk and disoriented, you could smell the alcohol on her breath. Her clothes were extremely sweaty, she was mumbling noises in her breath.

I was going to need to soften her up before I asked her about the form. I went in the kitchen to make some oatmeal for her breakfast, I made a bowl and brought it to her. She grumbled a thank you and clearly was not in the mood to speak, but I could tell she appreciated it. I went back to my room to kill time while I waited. I wasn't sure if she knew that the victim of the shooting yesterday had died, but I wasn't going to be the one to tell her.

Around the afternoon I tried again to see how Aunt Lala was feeling so I could bring up the good news, "Hey, it was something I was going to show you last night I think might cheer you up."

"Why didn't you show me last night?" she said, a slight tremble in her voice. I can tell she doesn't want me to see she's in an emotional state, but I don't think she realizes how she's coming across. Nonetheless, I realize she is going through something and this will make her feel better. I open the e-mail from Digital Records and show it to her. "You know what I can't stand about you Daniel?", this is not about to go the way I expected. "How's this random e-mail from a stranger supposed to make me feel better about Jay? How selfish are you that you think I would sign off on and travel with you while my son is in jail for something he didn't even do?", the trembling in her voice steadied as her anger grew.

"I didn't say any of that, I just showed you there's an opportunity that we can make money so Jay, Tasha, and I can all have better opportunities. I thought this was what you all *wanted* me to do. Now the opportunity is here so we can have a better life." I couldn't believe what was going on, so I just started explaining how we could use it to help Jay. "If we have money from this, we can pay for lawyer fees, we have money for him when he comes back home. You guys raised me to do this so we could live better, and I always did it with the intention to give back." Aunt Lala just looked at me like I had two heads, she was furious. I'm not going to sign this, Daniel, and I think you've overstayed your welcome here." She then pointed out to the door implied to leave.

My heart sunk in my chest. I worked so hard for so long, and the only reward I've earned is getting kicked out. It made absolutely zero sense. This can't be how the story ends. I swallow the saliva in my mouth and accept the situation while fighting back tears.

I walked towards my room to put together school bag and to start packing my clothes. "You're going the wrong way, stupid." She said as I went into my room. As I am still packing up my bag, she starts screaming "I SAID," she grabs me by the arm as I am putting my backpack on; "YOU'RE GOING THE WRONG WAY, YOU STUPID USELESS TWERP. GO SIGN THAT DEAL NOW," she throws me out and slams the door in on my face. I was in shock. Jay shoots someone and I get kicked out?

I go to the front of the complex and see one of Jays homies, SK. I asked him for his opinion on what happened. "The guy at the mall yesterday? He's the guy that took credit for shooting Smokey last week, he had to get him it was the only chance." Smokey was Jay's best friend from childhood, so I understood why Jay took it there. I understood why my aunt was in the mental state she was in about the situation, I already forgave them both for my own sake, but I still needed to figure out my next move. Knowing Jay just took someone out, it was in my best interest to get away from the neighborhood anyway.

I only had one other place to go at this moment, the gym. At the mall, you can run into anybody from anywhere at any moment, therefore it was the worst place to be when a war was going on. If I got to the gym safely though, I would be fine. I got on the bus wearing a covid mask, sunglasses, and a hoody. I didn't want anybody to make me until I was in the gym. I made sure to go straight to the back so I wouldn't have to worry about anyone sneaking up behind me.

I get off the bus and run as fast as I can to get to the gym. I walk in trying not to be seen at first thinking I can hold my belongings in the locker room. "Daniel, what is going on? Are you okay?" Jackie oversaw a lot of the youth programs at the gym, that's how she knows me Tay and Devon so well. "No, I'm not okay. Jay got arrested and I got kicked out." I told Jackie, almost in a whisper.

I was embarrassed about being homeless. It's alienating to lose the only identity I've ever had, my neighbourhood is the only place I felt like I belonged and that's gone now. Nothing made sense anymore. Repping a neighbourhood, no, willing to *die* and *kill* over a neighbourhood, where we don't even own property doesn't make sense.

"I need you to stay somewhere tonight," Jackie brings me into her office and makes a phone call. "Hey, I have a 15-year-old male here who was just kicked out of his home, is there space available?" I hear mumbling through the phone and Jackie starts speaking again, "What time does he need to be there by? He can be there within the hour." Jackie hangs up the phone and turns back to me, "Daniel, I need you to trust me right now. There is a youth shelter a few blocks away from here. They have a bed available, you'll need to share a room, but it's guaranteed that you'll have a roof over your head. Hopefully, you can get an apartment in a year. Just punch the address into your phone, head over. This is the best I can do for you right now."

Jackie was always a good-hearted person. She drove me to the shelter, and then I went inside to check it out. I was nervous, but I had to get ready for this next chapter of life.

Hello Michael,

I am very honoured and humbled that you reached out to me. Unfortunately, I don't know when I'll be able to travel. I hope you understand, and I hope to arrange something in the near future.

Blessings,

Crisis

Crisis,

After such a lengthy delay, your response comes as a surprise. All my years in the industry I have never seen a less enthusiastic, unhurried response.

Michael Williams, A&R

Digital Records

Chapter Two:
Stability

I tried to open the door but it was locked. Through the window, I could see an older lady with braids at reception. I tried to get her attention then I noticed the intercom. I pressed the button, it rings and she picks up. "May I have your name, please?" "Daniel Ibanez, aged 15." The door buzzes and I open it, she reaches out her hand to shake mine. "Cherise Goodwin," she gives me her name and shows me to my room.

"As you know, Jackie called on your behalf and we are here to help youth like you get yourselves stabilized. You'll be sharing a room with one roommate and if there's any problems, please just let us know." I get into the room and there is a bunkbed and two lockers, "Your roommates name is Kalief, he's out right now but will be back by our 1 A.M. curfew." I put my bags in the locker and followed Cherise back to her office for the intake process. Cherise pulls up her computer and points to a chair for me to take a seat. She boots it on and starts asking me questions about myself, starting with my birthday and how to spell my name.

"Just so you know, everything you tell me remains confidential. We just want to be properly aware of your situation so we can provide you with the right tools and assist to the best of our ability." Cherise assures me before getting personal, "I understand Miss." "Please call me Cherise, Miss is so formal" she says laughing to lighten the mood. "Are you registered for school next week?" "Yes, I'm starting grade 10 at Pope John Paul on Tuesday." "That's good, you guys got one heck of a ball team" "I know, me and Devon Carter are close friends."

Cherise's eyes glow up when she hears this; "That *is good*! So, you try to stay around the right crowd? That leads me to my next question, being that there are so many vulnerable youth in our community, I do need to ask you if you are a part of any gang?" I tell her, "My cousin was, but he's awaiting trial right now and his mom just kicked me out." "I am extremely sorry to hear that, how have you been processing it?", "I haven't had a chance to think about it, just trying to get my next moves sorted out first." Cherise nodded.

Cherise continued the questions, "Are you or do you have any history of self-medicating with any type of drugs or alcohol?" I respond calmly, "I always avoided them personally. I saw the effects alcohols had on people around me and never felt it was for me." Cherise looked at me very seriously and told me something profound; "You are smart. It would have been okay if you said yes because there is a reason why there is a liquor store in every plaza in our community, and it was so it would have the effect by which you have been traumatized. Alcohol comes from an Arabic word, Alkool, which means poison. It robs people of their conscience, morals, and plays an extremely pivotal role in making us to blame for our predicaments, they want us to poison ourselves and your futures."

I never sat down and thought about it that deeply before, but Cherise was completely right. Everybody I knew who engaged in the streets drank and/or smoked, everybody who had trouble at home with their family, it was usually fueled by alcohol. Now, I have someone who is seen countless situations like what I have borne witness to telling me that alcohol is as accessible as it is, so that it can create these problems for people. I took a moment to take in what Cherise was telling me, and it really made sense to me. I nodded agreeingly and allowed her to continue.

"All that's really left to fill out is an emergency contact. Are you okay with Jackie being your emergency contact for the time being?" Cherise asked, I nodded, and she filled out the last of the information needed. "There's one last question I need to ask you, are you good at cooking?" Cherise asked, "Yeah I can cook a little bit, how come?" I asked, "Well, it's almost dinner time, and it'll give you a chance to get settled in here for the night, and if you make it good, you might win some friends." Cherise joked around with me, and we went to the kitchen.

Cherise introduced me to the chef, who then gave me an apron and showed me a big pot of lentil soup. I start chopping up celery, carrots, and onions to go inside the soup, and then once I finish, I add them into the soup. The chef put a bunch of different spices and seasonings into it and then pointed to a bowl of dough. "I need you to take out little pieces of the flour and rub them in your hands together." I listened and made some dumplings to go into the soup. He gave me a sample at the end, it was amazing, I'm eating better here than I did at home.

It was a good system in place at the shelter, everybody who was staying there helped out in some way. Tonight, I was helping serve dinner, there were people cleaning up the kitchen, and others setting the table. I was extremely nervous to come here, I was nervous to be in a new place, but everybody seemed like they were just humble and trying to move forward in life. I felt a big sense of relief that things would be alright, at least for now.

Cherise pulls me to the side while serving dinner to introduce me to my roommate, "This is Kalief Wade, he's going to be your roommate while you stay here. I'll let you two get acquainted." Kalief was turning 19 soon and had been at the shelter for a year. First question he asks me was straight forward, "You look mad familiar, where do I know you from?"

This is a question that could always go one of two ways; Somewhere good, or somewhere bad. My intuition was to just be real and respectful, "I don't know where we would have met to be honest, but I'm from Eastside." Something clicked in Kalief's head, "You're Crisis, right? You have that one song everyone's been playing in the city!"

Once Kalief said that it was like my cover was blown. My goal was to be here and not make too much noise or draw any attention to myself, now that seems unlikely. "You got mad talent, man, you next up from the city for sure. But how you end up in here? Call me Leaf by the way." Leaf had good intentions and wasn't trying to put me on blast, he just got excited. I didn't want to make a problem where there wasn't one, so I kept it real, "My aunt was tripping on me, so I had to move out." Leaf kissed his teeth, then said "Family can be the worst people to you sometimes, man, sorry to hear that."

After dinner, me and Leaf went back to our room and he pulled out a giant wad of cash. It looked like it was at least two thousand dollars, all in hundreds. He casually started counting it. I had to ask him, "What you got going on fam? I got to get like you." Leaf looked back over at me and grinned, "Young Crisis wants to join the team? I was just down the street at the bar, bare customers." Leaf continued, "When they clear us for the night, I'll tell them I'm bringing you out to see the neighborhood, as long as you're with me you're going to be alright trust me."

"I need to know what I'm getting myself into first though, what kind of customers?" I asked Leaf, "You're a rapper, right? This is that Get Rich or Die Trying lifestyle, I been trapping out of here since I got here. You roll with me, you can make all the money and avoid all the hood politics, how does that sound?" It sounded like the deal of the century, it almost sounded as good as the record deal.

"Okay I'm down to check it out." I gave Leaf a dap. It was around 9pm, so we had 4 hours to go back down the street and he took me to the bar. I'm thinking there's no way they're going to let me sit at the bar and drink, I am only five foot five and 120 pounds, and clearly underage. We arrive and settle in two stools at the bar, Leaf gets himself a rum and coke and orders me a ginger ale. Turns out the staff doesn't care I'm there, regardless of my age.

"You don't drink, Crisis?" Leaf asks "Not really my thing, I don't knock anybody for it though," I tell him. I can tell he's trying to get to know me, he continues on the subject, "Is there a reason in particular or just not really feeling it?" I know Leaf is the main person I'm going to need to learn to trust, but I just met him, and I don't want to speak ill of my family.

"There's a reason why, but I can't tell you what it is right now, respectfully." Is my eventual answer to Leaf. Leaf laughs, "I respect it." he shrugs and lifts his glass. He takes a sip and leans into me to tell me something quietly over the loud music, "it's too late for me bro, but you, you got an advantage by not drinking. Anytime we go out, you can be the reliable designated driver. Having a clear head while you are out in the streets can make you more on point, and more cautious of the police or opposition. You're going to be able to see things happening long before they happen, and that's important to stay safe out here."

An older white male approached Leaf and gave him a dap and then a hug. He was balding, had dark bags under his eyes, and wore all black. They have an exchange and Leaf points to me. He gives me a dap too, then walks away. "He just bought off of you?" I ask Leaf. He looks at me and says, "No, he just bought off of you!" and then hands me $120 in twenties. Leaf continued, "you roll with me, I'm going to make sure you live a good life. I might not be able to give you a record deal, but what I can do, is show you how to get money for yourself. Then, you can build your own opportunities, be your own man., We got a bright future working together. Only question left to ask, is are you in?"

I looked around, I needed a moment to answer. I just made 120 dollars just by sitting down at a bar, and school starting next week. I give Leaf a dap and tell him, "I'm in. Let us get this money." Ten minutes pass and the same guy from earlier comes back with another person, an older white woman with biker clothes, a lot of makeup, and a messy red hair. This time they came up to me with $240, then gave Leaf props and went back to their table.

I haven't touched anything yet, or even know what it is they are buying off us. Leaf gets up, puts a bag of something in my pocket, he tells me, "Don't look at it yet," then goes to the washroom. I put my hand in my pocket to feel what was inside, it was a plastic resealable bag containing smaller bags. The texture of whatever was in the smaller bags felt smooth but had some chunks depending on where I felt. I know it's drugs, but I have no way to tell what kind until I can go to the washroom and look. Leaf comes back and I get up to go to the washroom.

I walk through the men's room door, luckily it's just one toilet with a sink. I can lock the door and nobody will know what I am up to. I take the bag out to look, it's a white powder with sparkles inside of it. Cocaine. About four bags of it. I started today with nothing, now I'm holding $360, assuming each bag is worth $120. I check my phone to see the time, it's only 10pm. I see texts from my sister, Mimi, and Devon, but they have to wait. I might be able to end tonight with $840, and I was going to make sure that I did.

I go back to the bar and see Leaf. Surprisingly, I see SK from the block with him. "You two know each other?" SK says in disbelief, Leaf explains to him, "Crisis, might be our new employee," Leaf turns to me, "You owe me $400 for that bag and there's 3 hours on the clock. Can you pay it off in time?" I nod and ask, "who can I ask here to buy?" Leaf turns his head and shows me who is open to talk to, he points to a group of five guys sitting down at a table. Leaf gives me the play "You see the pitcher they are sharing? You might not have noticed, but that's their fifth tonight. All of them are drunk, and they have clear vices. In 5 minutes, one of them will come up to the bar and order another pitcher, when he comes here, you introduce yourself."

I give it some time and wait. One guy gets up and walks towards the bar, Leaf calls out to him, "you guys are turning up over there!" the guy laughs and says, "this isn't even the real party pal!" He stops to talk to us while he waits for the next pitcher, "What would make it the real party?" Leaf asks him. "You know what we need! You got it or not?" Leaf nudges his head in my direction. "I want 4 grams of your best product, sir!" He says to me laughing. I gave him the rest of the bags and he hands me almost $500, I give $400 to Leaf. Leaf gets me another ginger ale, rum and coke for himself, and a gin and juice for SK. They both raise their glasses and we cheers, "You're hired!!!!"

Leaf and SK head out for a smoke break, I head out too since we've finished our drinks. I count out what I made in front of them, it was a total of $440. Leaf gives me a choice to make, "You can give me $400, get the next bag to sell tomorrow, or we can keep it on consignment. Which would you prefer?" I don't think I've ever made this much money this easily before. With Jay and his friends, we would commit petty crimes and steal little things here and there, but it was never anything like this. This could be done easily, under the radar, every day.

I know I'm coming back to the bar tomorrow night after I finish work, so I decided to give Leaf $400 for the next bag. Leaf breaks everything down for me, "This is a quarter ounce. It is seven grams total, all bagged out into grams, and each gram costs $120. You don't let anybody try to get a discount or a lower amount, its 120 a gram minimum or they get nothing, got

24

it?" I nod my head and we give each other a dap. SK stays at the bar, me and Leaf head back down the street to the shelter.

I started checking my phone as we were walking, I felt like I needed to get back to everybody. Leaf presses the intercom at the door and Cherise buzzes us in. "Did you two have a fun evening?" Cherise asked, Leaf responded, "yeah just showing my new roomie the neighborhood," Cherise asks if I had a good night "Yeah, but I'm tired now," I said. "That's good, just stay out of trouble you two!!". I have no idea if she has any clue what Leaf's been up to his whole time here, but I didn't want to risk saying the wrong thing. We got back to our room, I plugged in my phone and checked my texts.

Devon Carter: *(9:05pm)*

Yo fam you reaching the gym tomorrow?

Me: *(12:08am)*

Yes bro I will be there early, but not to play ball. Sorry for the late reply.

Natasha Ibanez: *(8:18pm)*

Hey Daniel, worried, can you let me know where you are? I will not tell Auntie just need to know for myself you are okay…

Natasha Ibanez: *(9:00pm)*

Daniel, please respond, just let me know you are safe. I hope you are not mad at me too. This is worrying.

Me: *(12:12am)*

Hey sis, I am fine. Sorry for the late reply was just out late. I am staying at a shelter on Eglinton Avenue a couple of blocks away from the house, I am safe and have a job interview tomorrow. No need to worry.

Natasha Ibanez: *(12:13am)*

Thank God, I am really sorry you are going through this, just stay connected. I will make sure you are out of there in no time just get some rest for now and focus on tomorrow. Love you bro!

Me: *(12:14am)*

Love you too sis, have a goodnight.

Mimi Singh: *(9:15pm)*

Hey! Your sister messaged me asking if I heard from you, are you okay?

Mimi Singh: *(9:30pm)*

Daniel, you are scaring us. Where are you and are you okay?

Mimi Singh: *(10:48pm)*

Daniel, please text me or call me as soon as possible. This is extremely important, I can't be this far away not knowing whether you are safe or not, please understand that and get back to me or your sister asap.

Me: *(12:16am)*

Hey babe, I am really sorry for the late replies, I was out all day and didn't have a chance to check my phone. I really wanted you to hear this from me first, but my aunt kicked me out this morning, she is still really shaken up about Jay. I am staying at a youth shelter for the time being and have a job interview tomorrow at the gym I always go to. I will be okay, and I am really sorry you were worried; it wasn't my intention.

Mimi Singh: *(12:17am)*

Omg thank God there is no need to be sorry Daniel just was worried. You told me nothing changes between us, right? I trust you I just want you to be safe where you are and stay connected with me, okay?

Me: *(12:18am)*

I am really grateful to you Mimi, and exactly, I love you and I am going to be safe. Rest well, okay?

Mimi Singh: *(12:18am)*

I love you too Daniel, you are the strongest person I know, and you are going to get through this. Goodnight!

Getting back to everybody made me realize I have a lot of people around who care about me. People would really be hurt if something happened to me. How would they cope if I got shot or arrested? On the other hand, I don't have many options but to get myself stabilized, as fast as possible. I am going to need money to buy a car, money to invest in music, money to travel, and get myself a place to live. The fact is, I do need to take the risk of selling drugs, but I need to be smart about it.

I still had to head to school to get my timetable. I was hoping the earlier I went in, the fewer people I would need to see. Orientation was yesterday, but obviously other things were taking up my time. I didn't want to explain myself to anybody when I went in, just get the schedule and go back to the shelter. I got to the school and saw the admin, Susanna Caruso. Susanna was an older lady that would always wear glasses and had long curly hair.

"Where were you yesterday, mister?" Susanna asked me. "It's a long story that I don't really want to get into right now, but I'd like to pick up my schedule for Tuesday." I told her, she replied, "Is everything okay? Is there it anything we can help you out with?" I told her, "Not right now, just need to put my focus into school." Susanna smiled and agreed. She printed out the schedule and I was on my way back to the shelter.

I got back around 2pm and decided to take it easy for the rest of the day. I might go to the bar with Leaf later, but I have a lot to think about. I am starting Grade 10 with a job, the girl I love is in another country, and I must turn down the record deal I don't know where life is taking me, but I need to be ready for the journey. Life has given me my cards; I can play them.

Chapter Three:
The Party

It's the first day of school, I have my uniform ready to go; All black unmarked dress shoes, grey slacks, and a navy-blue polo shirt with my school's crest on the side. Since Scarborough is a diverse city, the shelter needs to make sure to provide food everyone can eat. All vegan, zero potential allergens, nothing that would restrict someone from eating. This meant breakfast would usually be cornmeal porridge, luckily for me, that was my favourite. I got ready as soon as I finished, I needed to make a good impression on the first day.

I catch the bus to school and check my timetable, I got history first period, English second period, math in third, and science last. My history teacher's name is, Mr. Hadi. He's new, so I don't know what to expect until I get there. For English I have Ms. Caruso. Because of budget cuts she had to help admin as well as the English teacher. I got the same math teacher that I had last year, Mrs. Monet. She was my favorite teacher last year so this is a relief. For science I have another new teacher, Mr. Iglesias, which was ironic to anybody fluent in Spanish.

I arrive early and go to first period. Mr. Hadi checks my schedule and shakes my hand to welcome me. Mr. Hadi wasn't what I expected, he was a young Black teacher starting his first full time teaching position, 25 years old at most. There were pictures of prominent leaders like Malcolm X, Muhammad Ali, John Carlos, covering the walls of the classroom. I had a good feeling about what I would learn in this class. He started a

29

conversation with me, "Do you usually show up to school early. Or just on late start days?"

I knew it was a joke, so I answered laughing, "I do my best to be my best in every possible situation. I don't count the days, I make the days count." Mr. Hadi noticed me staring at the Muhammad Ali picture, he was impressed, "Are you familiar with Muhammad Ali, Daniel?" I responded, "He's the greatest boxer of all time, my dad taught me all about him, Malcolm X, and the Black Panthers."

"That's amazing, what was his take on them?" Mr. Hadi inquired. "My father was a die-hard Muhammad Ali fan and was always a big supporter of the liberation movement. He told me how Martin Luther King and Malcolm X had different ideologies on how to achieve freedom but needed each other to make progress." Mr. Hadi was blown away and told me, "Before anybody comes up in here, you are going to be my favorite student, I'm very excited to be your teacher."

Second period starts, and I see Ms. Caruso sitting down. The classroom is full and there are only two seats available, so I take a seat in one. Beside me is Jason Jackson, he's been my classmate since elementary school. He went by Snipa now. He's from the same neighborhood as me, but on the other side, the Bloods side. We haven't really been friends since Grade six. Once I realized where I sat, I got right back up and chose the other seat.

I got to the third period, Mrs. Monet is there and the class is smaller than I expected, about 15 students maximum. Devon's in this class with me, so I sat next to him. Mrs. Monet broke down the syllabus and offered resources to make sure everybody in the class was able to keep up. If there were more teachers like Mrs. Monet, more teenagers would take school seriously. You can only reciprocate respect when it's given, and when an authority figure shows they care about you, it's easier to care about what they're teaching.

I knew I had absolutely zero future in the field of science and didn't even want to go into school in the first place, so I skipped Mr. Iglesias' orientation. Even if chemistry might be involved in my new career path, it's not in my paygrade to oversee production. The game plan was simple, pass every class, go to work every day, and put the money into my *real* future.

I go outside the school and see Leaf in a new car blasting music. It was a brand new, royal blue, Lexus RX, with limo tinted windows. He points to the back seat, so I open the door behind him and get in the car. It has white leather seats and still has the new car smell. I look up and to my surprise, beside Leaf in the passenger seat was the same girl from the mall that rejected Tay. "Crisis, this is my girl, Lacey."

I shook her hand, and she started a conversation, "Hey kid, I've seen you around somewhere before, haven't I?" I didn't want the intro to be that my friend was trying to pick her up a week ago, but thankfully before I could make up a story Leaf goes into full big brother mode, "Everybody seen Crisis somewhere before! This is the next big artist out the city!" he declared and then started playing my song.

Leaf picks up SK, then we just drive around selling to anybody who calls one of our phones. We got back to my old block and parked outside SK's house, he got in and dapped everybody up. He told us he had a play for us, "Friday night, it's a party over by the mall, we got to be there guys." Leaf got excited, "how many people do you thinks going to be there?" "All of Scarborough is going to be at this party, we can't afford to miss this," SK replied.

Leaf got nervous after hearing that, "That's worrying, bro. I don't like being around people from different hoods at the same time. Just problems waiting to happen." SK refuted, "It's not going to be one of those, bro, it's high school and college kids, no politics." "They always advertise them like that" Leaf laughed and continued, "I don't have time for something to go wrong right now."

One thing I respected about Leaf, is he was laser focused on success. Leaf was somebody who knew how to stay completely out of the way and focus solely on what mattered, which was making money and getting away from the problems. If there was any chance of police being somewhere, he had the discipline to just not go. SK on the other hand, he just wanted to be around as much fun as possible. Party, drink, and fight. He moved dangerously, but the duality between them made them perfect business partners.

As the week progressed, Leaf's mind opened more about going to the party. He made a deal with SK, the second something seems like it could escalate, we leave. I woke up Friday with an eerie feeling, but I knew I wanted to get paid today. I get to Mr. Hadi's class early every day to talk to him before class starts.

I was learning so much from him, like this concept called "systematic oppression," you strip one tribe of the resources needed for stability, and that tribe has no choice but to find a way around their circumstance. Then, you build laws and legislations to prohibit their solution; Now that tribe is forced into survival mode. Once the brain is in survival mode, it becomes toxic and jaded, willing to destroy itself and its own community for the sake of its individual survival.

I ended up going to Mr. Iglesias' class eventually and he was cool too. He was an older teacher, came from another school, has 10 years left before retirement, tops. I apologized to him for missing the orientation, and he didn't seem to mind at all. He just wanted me to make sure I stayed on top of the assignments and passed my tests. I was at the lab desk waiting for the bell to ring, he could tell, and he understood that there are a lot of students just there for the credit.

School was done for the weekend, and I rushed downstairs to see Leaf, SK and Lacey in the Lexus waiting. I felt a push from behind on my right shoulder and heard Snipas voice, "Smokey's still in hell and now Jay's in jail getting back shots." SK saw the altercation, hopped out of the car and approached Snipa, "Don't ever let me see you do that again!" Snipa laughed at SK and said "You want to fight a 14-year-old? This is why Eastside's the lamest hood ever. Go back to your buddy's car you loser. You're not going to touch me on school property." Me and SK let him go for now, there was too much to lose.

We got ready for the party, Leaf was adamant that he didn't want any problems, so I made sure I did my part. I wore the classic dope boy party outfit; Black hoodie, black jeans, black Jordans, with a black Toronto Blue Jays fitted to match. SK wore a black hoodie with some black Chuck Taylors, and Leaf wore a black varsity jacket with black air-forces. We dressed as a unit. Me and SK might have been from the Eastside, but we were committed to something else right now.

We arrived at the party early, SK made sure we would be the only people allowed to serve in there, anybody else would be forced to leave. The party wasn't far from Tay's house, so I knew he and Devon would be attending. I told Devon during lunch this week what happened at home, but I didn't tell him or Tay that I'm selling drugs now. There was a strong chance they would both find out tonight, and I don't have time to worry about what they think.

Snipa and some of his friends show up to the party. He had an older friend, Shotty, in grade 12 who went to another school. Shotty's best friend, Fredo, was there too. He was the same age as Shotty and went to the same school as him. The trio instantly gave me, SK, and Leaf dirty looks the moment they saw us. This was a bad sign, but if they had no intentions of starting a problem, neither did we. They started pouring their drinks and faded away shortly after, and we just focused on what we came to do. At any public event you need to leave all the problems at the door.

After an hour I heard a muffled voice; "How much for a gram?" I turned around and I saw Tay and Devon laughing. They figured it out, but it seemed like they didn't care. I know Tay expected it to happen eventually before the context of getting kicked out. I know they both have a lot to lose, I didn't want my problems to bleed into their paths and make it harder for them.

Tonight is a special night for me, Leaf moved me up to a half-ounce. I paid half of it up-front and need to pay the second half to him when I sell out. If we keep up the pace, hopefully I'll move up to a full ounce by the end of the month. Things were going up slowly but surely, and after about two hours into the party it looked like I was going to be able to make enough to pay Leaf. Currently, I'm only $200 short. It starts feeling hot in the house because there are so many people people, so I go out to get some air. I see Tay outside sharing a blunt with a girl from the party, and when they see me. Tay gives her a look to say he'll meet her inside, it's clear he wants to talk.

"Before you say anything, man, I get it, but I don't think I can hang around you as often anymore. I told you this was coming." Tay said disappointed and continued, "You're still one of my best friends for life Crise, and any situation you need a friend to talk to I'm there, but you know I can't be getting involved or associated with anything like that." Once he was done, I was disappointed too, but it was relieving that it's out of the way. "I was worried about what y'all would say. The last thing I would ever want is for you all winding up in this mess with me. This won't be my life forever, hopefully we can spend time together when I'm out of this.." I told Tay, and he really looked at me the same way that he did back at the mall.

"You still don't get it; you're putting yourself deeper in the situation, Crisis. If you get caught, you're going to miss *at least*

34

a month of school. How would you catch up? The answer is you will not, you're going to need to repeat your classes, and that's cool for you if you don't want to go to college. Devon is going to get a scholarship to a good college against a million kids applying for the same thing, imagine if he had to miss school for being guilty by association to you. I really hope you do get out of this Crisis, I'm going to miss hanging out with you until you do."

That last sentence from Tay hurt bad, I really started seeing how I was stuck in a tricky situation. The reality is I am going through something Tay and Devon are not going through themselves, and they can't understand why I would need to take this route. I'm realizing I have to accept there will be more distance between myself and the people I care about the most. First it was Mimi, then my family, now my best friends. Mimi's physically at distance, now my best friends are metaphorically at a distance. I was telling myself the same thing I did by the water with Mimi; real bonds are releasable, and nothing real can break. The void hurts more than I expected.

I stayed outside and got lost in a trance thinking of memories with Mimi, Devon, and Tay. I even felt like drinking, everyone says it helps you go numb and move on. Before I could turn around to go back inside, I hear a gun being cocked, then I feel something extremely cold like metal touching the side of my face. I look to the side and see Snipa, Shotty, and Fredo surrounding me. Snipa is holding the gun, but he's not looking at me, his eyes arc to the ground; He doesn't want to do it.

Fredo pushes Snipa, "Get him gone don't waste time." I felt the steel shaking against my temple, but he couldn't bring himself to pull the trigger. I was strictly there for profit, Leaf felt no need to make sure I had a weapon on me, because it would have been two charges to have the drugs and a gun on my person if things went wrong. I had cash and drugs in my pocket, I was worried they were going to take everything I made tonight. I realize in this moment, I am more worried about the money than my life. Snipa speaks up after a moment, "It's too hot here, just run his pockets," Shotta kisses his teeth and reaches for the pocket. Right before he could fit his hand inside, six shots ring in my eardrum. For a second, I thought I was dead, instead, I see Snipa looking toward the ground, the gun out of his hand and scattered out of reach. Fredo and Shotty are on the ground on either side of Snipa.

Fredo was wearing a white shirt, a red stain that kept growing, consuming more of his shirt. Shotty had blood coming out of his Jeans and his arm. I am processing what it is that just happened in front of me, I hear SK screaming; "WHAT ARE YOU DOING CRISIS WE GOTTA GO!" SK shot them to save my life. Me and SK rush to the Lexus, Leaf and Lacey are already inside. Leaf peels off, it felt like he went from zero to one hundred in a second. My heart is pumping right now like it never has before, somebody just tried to take my life away from me, and now I am involved in a double or even triple murder, and what were Snipa's intentions?

I was trying to piece it together, Snipa is an old friend turned enemy for reasons that really had nothing to do with us. Was he hoping he could convince his friends to just rob me and let me live? Was he starting to regret the decision to enter his gang? If I were somebody else, would it have been a different outcome? I don't know what kind of situation I'm in yet, but I know I can't get myself out. Snipa, Shotty, and Fredo are in an unknown condition and everybody at the party knows me, Leaf, and SK, bolted right after. Me and Leaf must go back to the shelter like nothing happened and I need to go to the same class as Snipa on Monday. This is not going to end well.

Leaf is fuming, he kept insisting not to go to the party for the sole purpose of avoiding a situation where police could get involved. We weren't even there for three hours, and we did exactly that. "All I said was let's make sure there's no problems, all we had to do wasn't shoot anybody!" Leaf huffed; "Did we even make a thousand dollars in total tonight, what was the point of that?" he continued. SK eventually interjected, "Crisis could've got killed, what was I supposed to do?" Leaf got madder, "Call their bluff!! At absolute most pull out and see if they stop. You didn't need to do that, man. This is why I don't like bringing you to these places."

Leaf drove Lacey to her house, she gave him a kiss and went inside, as SK gets out to go into the front seat Leaf stops him; "Get your ass back in there now, we're not done I'm just getting started with you." Leaf gets back in the driver's seat and continues, "I am not going to tolerate this Crips vs Bloods 1990s retro vengeance bullshit. I signed up to get money. You signed up to get money. Crisis signed up to get money, he is just starting and can't afford fuck ups like this. Crisis has to go to school with that kid, why the hell would he really shoot? You can't jump the gun like that because come Monday, the first person who has to talk to the police is going to be the person you were protecting, SK! Don't do nothing dumb like this again!"

Leaf makes me get in the front seat when we get to SK's house, then he tells me what to do. "So, I know this is scary and not how you wanted tonight to go, but we're in the situation, and we need to handle this accordingly. There is a best-case scenario, and a worst-case scenario right now. Best-case scenario, they're alive, no one made the car or realized you were involved, and nobody even comes to question us, we get away Scott-free. But you still got to be ready for whatever Snipa might pull. Worst-case scenario, someone is dead, the police know we are involved, and I need to say what I need to say, and you need to say what I need to say. We need to have the story straight from now, because we might not have another chance to put it together."

Leaf told me the script; "My story is that I was in my car, and I was your ride to the party. When the shots got fired, you ran to the car, and we drove away to safety. Your story is you were outside getting fresh air, you were standing on the other side of the balcony when you heard the shots. You didn't know what happened, so you ran to the car and we both went back to the shelter. We're on curfew so we needed to leave soon anyway. No matter what, you didn't pull the trigger and you are technically innocent in all of this, and I'm technically innocent in all of this, neither of us shot anyone. We should be safe, but I need you to prove something to me with how you handle this situation."

We got back to the shelter and checked in, then went straight to our room. The very first thing I did was check the news on my phone. I searched up *shooting in Scarborough tonight* on incognito mode and to see what would pop up. My palms are sweating like crazy as my phone is loading. The first thing I see is breaking news; it just got reported.

A back-to-school party in Central Scarborough tonight ends with a youth unable to graduate, leaving the community in mourning. Two teenagers, Frederick Daniels (17), and Eric Arthur (18), were shot. Luckily, Brandon only suffered minor injuries and is expected to make a full recovery. Frederick however, unfortunately died at the scene before Paramedics were able to arrive. Frederick is remembered by his mother and siblings as misunderstood, but a very good-hearted kid with ambitions of going to college and becoming a journalist.

There are currently no suspects or leads at this time, Toronto Police Service and Frederick's family are asking for anybody with information to come forward.

I should have felt relief reading that, but I didn't. Snipa was never hit so he is going to be at school on Monday, furious about what happened. I needed to live with the fact that for as long as I live, I am the reason someone is not in this realm anymore. Sometimes, you can be lucky and have no evidence against you, you can get off on a technicality, but the energy stays no matter what. Whatever is put out into the universe will always return to you.

Me: *(12:01am)*

Please tell me you are awake right now...

Mimi Singh: *(12:01am)*

Lol its Friday night! Of course, I am, are you okay?

Me: *(12:02am)*

I wish I were. Things are really messed up for me out here. It keeps going from bad to, worse, to even worse than what I even thought possible. I don't know how I thought this year was going to go, but I definitely didn't expect this.

Mimi Singh: *(12:03am)*

I am so sorry you are going through this babe, believe me, I hate it where I am too. It is so hot for no reason, it is impossible for me to make friends. The girls hate me just because a popular girl told them to, I would do anything to come back.

Me: *(12:04am)*

I don't even think staying here is going to be a possibility much longer, but wherever I go or end up, I really can't stand my life without you. I need you. I love you. I need to protect you from my situation right now, but I promise you this is not going to be it for me. I am going to get the things I need, get back to music, and we're going to buy a house somewhere nice and start our family. I told you nothing changes between us, and I am holding myself to that.

Mimi Singh: *(12:05am)*

I love you too Daniel, I really do. And trust me, you have no idea how much I wish you were here. I think about you all the time, I worry about you all the time too. I keep having flashbacks of that day by the water, to us playing truth or dare, to us kissing. I keep remembering the first time I saw you perform and fell in love with you. What you are going through back home is going to be a testament to your story, to our story, and is going to inspire millions of people just like you, who had to overcome the same obstacles and found a way to do it. When we get past this, all of it is going to have been worth it. I am still right beside you in spirit, and I will always be here for you.

Me: *(12:06am)*

I am so grateful for you for real babe, you have no idea how lifesaving this conversation felt. I have got a long week ahead of me, and I don't know how it is going to end, but no matter what happens I love you forever and whatever it takes we are going to make this work. Have a goodnight, babe sweet dreams.

Mimi Singh: *(12:06am)*

Goodnight baby sweet dreams to you too and I love you too! We are making it through this!

Chapter Four:

Loyalty

I wake up and look at my phone, it's 4:00am on Monday morning. The same time I've been waking up every morning since it happened. I can't remember the last time I ate, but it was before the party. I was going to need to face Snipa today in class, I have don't know what to expect. The reality is I really shouldn't feel bad; I was leaving him and his friends completely alone. Fredo would still be here if they didn't feel the need to rob me. On top of that, the whole time I was there, it was understood I was just a kid doing music with the intention to make it out of there.

I left the shelter early for school. I was hoping if I got to Mr. Hadi's class before anybody even got to school and skipped second period, I could avoid any problems before lunch. The second I got outside I noticed a black Dodge Durango in the distance with the lights on. The car looked familiar too, but I couldn't make where it was from. I looked towards the bus stop, and then I looked back at the Durango, and could sense what might happen. I couldn't spend my life living in fear for something that truthfully wasn't my fault. I start to walk slowly towards the bus stop hoping that the bus won't be long. I sit down on the bench by the stop and check the time it's coming, it says five minutes.

I try my hardest not to look directly at the car down the street, so I rely on my peripheral vision to see if it's coming towards me; it's not. The car is staying still with the lights on running, I start to question myself and begin to assume that the car has nothing to do with me. For all that I know, it could be someone just waiting for someone else to carpool to work. I start to relax, I go on my phone to text my friends and check social media. The bus comes so I get on to find a seat and start the day.

I reach my school, Mr. Hadi and most of the teachers are not there yet. The only staff members on site currently are the custodian, making sure the water is clean, and the Track-and-Field coach, doing the first practice of the season. I decided my best bet right now is to join them on their run to kill the time. Devon was there taking the extra step to help him with his game, as most athletes do. I started running with him. The drill was to jog from school to a nearby park a few blocks over and then back to the school. This gave me a chance to talk to somebody to see what everybody is saying about the situation.

Devon's first question caught me completely off guard; "Did you hear what happened on Friday?" If my best friend had no idea I engaged in the shooting, it had to mean that I was really in the clear from any legal issues, but I wasn't about to lie to Devon either. "Yeah of course, I saw it happen, that's why I left." Devon shook his head while jogging, "I am not going to switch on you like Tay did, but if I'm staying loyal to you, you got to make sure you are not going to let yourself get killed or sent to juvie, because then I have to cope with that. Those older dudes you have been hanging with, they are not going to tell you this but if something goes wrong you know you are the only one out of them that is underage, that means it will be easy to let you take a charge for them."

I can't lie, I didn't consider that Leaf could play that card with me if things went wrong, now I'm questioning everything. I told Devon what I felt was the truth to assure him, but as I was saying it I felt as if I was assuring myself too, "Leaf didn't want us to attend that party for the specific reason that something could have gone wrong. He's been a good mentor and makes sure I stay safe. As soon as trouble started, he kept his word and made sure we got right out of there." Devon looked slightly relieved but still wanted me to be careful about my own well-being. "Just be careful Crisis, you've got a lot to lose too."

After the speech Tay gave me about how we are no longer spending time together because he can't afford to let his grades slip or get in trouble, he still found the time to text me this morning asking to buy a half-gram. Meanwhile, Devon has college scholarship scouts looking at him and needs a clean image. Devon is the one who has decided to not let my situation affect our friendship, because he knows that I wouldn't let anything happen to him. Mine and Devon's brotherhood was sacred, and we were going to be on top of the world together one day.

The track team did some stretches, there was still about a half hour before classes started, so Mr. Hadi had to be in his classroom by now. I go there to see the door open, and he is staring me right in the eyes before I even walk through it. I go to my seat without saying anything, and he just gets up and closes the door. "Daniel, do you trust me?" he asks me in a low and calm voice, "Yes sir, of course I do." I respond in the same calm manner, and he asks me, "Did you watch the news at all this weekend by any chance?"

My heart sank. Shotty and Fredo were not even students at this school, the only person he could know about wasn't arrested or injured, so how could this news reach him, unless... Unless Mr. Hadi is a retired member and knows about the beef. I still wasn't sure if he knew I knew about it, but I still had to play it safe. "Mr. Hadi, what is this about exactly?" Mr. Hadi sat down beside me, putting his hand on my shoulder and explains; "I grew up down the street from you, I knew you were going to the party, and I knew Frederick's mom before the neighborhood separated."

Mr. Hadi continued; "Look around the classroom, you have got to know the last thing I would ever do is cooperate with the police. I am here as someone who is double your age, who wants to see you make it out of this vicious cycle. I wasn't always this aware of the world around me, I let you come in early to class so I can give you the game because I wish I had someone to explain it to me before it was too late. I can tell just by you walking through that door early every day, you desire a better life and a better future. You don't need to tell me anything you are uncomfortable with me knowing, I don't want a confession from you. I want you to understand that I know you did the right thing."

"The story I was told is, they were trying you and you didn't give anything up, but you didn't instigate or make the situation what it was. Jason, Snipa, you two both attended elementary school together, am I correct? Just six years ago, when you two were eight or nine years old, this division started. It wasn't over anything noble; it was because of a girl who was dating two different guys at the same time. One shot the other, then after three retaliations later, the initial problem didn't even matter anymore."

"My cousin Jay told me his big homie got robbed for a brick, and then he shot in self-defense." Mr. Hadi wanted to laugh but couldn't; the pain of the memories started hitting him too, "Classic case of male ego, your cousin didn't lie to you, your cousin was lied to. My guess is, Fleet didn't want to admit a girl played him and felt your cousin wouldn't have taken him seriously of as a leader if he said what it was really about. Once that amount of blood that has been spilled, people don't really care about the real reason why.

"It became convenient to blame the other side for everything, and then even easier to steal from them to feed our own side.(A low income neighbourhood...). It is the exact example of the divide and conquer method I have taught you; Pit two groups against each other and make them fight each other, distracting them from their true oppressor, and in turn making them take each other out. Then, that same oppressive force keeps its hands

44

clean in the process. Everybody you know who has either lost their life on the streets, or has been put behind bars, it was all to help billionaires and politicians we will never even meet. That is why nobody steps in and calls for peace because capitalism benefits from this continuing."

"That is why having someone like you, who can rep Scarborough in a positive light and be the force to invest in our neighborhoods is so crucial. You have a lot of gifts, Daniel, and that attracts a lot of envy and evil eyes. You might not be ready to hear this, but it is part of why your aunt kicked you out, you are over here getting record contracts while her son is being sent to jail for murder. She wanted your blessings for him, but she had no way to even begin trying to express that, especially knowing how wrong it is. That's why no matter how gloomy and dark your situation looks right now, you must keep pushing through, there is so much more than the streets you need to overcome in life, Daniel."

Mr. Hadi knew I needed to hear that. He didn't care about his job or being fired; He knew that speech was needed so he gave it. I ended up going to second period, and Snipa was present. He was staring me down whenever he felt like I wasn't looking. That's when it hit me; I recognized the Durango from when Snipa's mom used to drive him to school. It was him in the car, but if he had the chance to get me, why would he not?

Snipa has always been a troublemaker and always instigated fights when he saw fit, but this felt different. Usually, he would say disrespectful things to whoever and brag about himself to prove how he is better than whoever else. This time he was just focused and not saying anything. It was a completely different version of him that had never been seen before. I didn't know whether to feel bad or just amp it up, but I was getting sick of it.

"Yo watch your own book, stop staring at me." I finally said to Snipa, and he snapped. He got right out of his seat and was ready to fight in the classroom. "Are you dumb? Who do you think you're talking to you homeless bum? Get out of here!" Ms. Caruso tried to stand between the middle of us to stop the fight before it happened, one of our classmates ran out to get help. "You're not even Eastside anymore to even want to beef with anybody, you gotta rep the Shelter boys now you wasteman, don't ever try that again."

We both got sent to the principal's office, both of us were fuming and they made sure to keep us in separate rooms. I was with the vice principal, Snipa was with the principal, we both knew neither of us were going to admit to what the fight was about otherwise the police would automatically get involved in the situation. The vice principal asked me, "What was this about Daniel?" I responded politely, "I don't like being stared at" The vice principal shook her head up and down understanding and responded, "That's fair but did it need to explode into this big of an issue?" I swallowed my pride and agreed, "You're right, we took it too far."

The principal brought Snipa into the room, he was a lot less angry than before but still visibly frustrated. The principal spoke to me, "Jason says that he didn't understand why you randomly yelled at him in class, and it triggered him." The Vice Principal chimed in with my side of the story; "Daniel thought Jason was staring at him. Can we chop this up to a misunderstanding and get back to class?" Me and Snipa were still very mad at each other, but we both knew the best thing we could do was pretend to resolve it, so no further questions were asked. We apologized to each other, shook hands, and went back to class.

I wasn't happy about it, but it was the smartest thing to do. The truth is, it didn't matter, I didn't do anything wrong, but Snipa was going through a grieving process. I wish sometimes that we could have just stayed cool, and the neighborhood problems wouldn't have affected us being cordial with each other, but Snipa wanted to be down. That is just what it was with him, and I just needed to keep my eyes peeled and be careful, get through the day, and get home.

I start to head to the bus station, and see the Durango parked in the distance again. Now I know for sure Snipa is using his mom's car to stalk me, He is making sure he knows when I go to school, when I leave, and when I check in at the shelter. My guess is that he is planning to kill me in retaliation for Fredo. I don't respect it at all, but I know better than to take it personal; We are two youths in survival mode because of issues bigger than the both of us.

I get back to the shelter and hope I can talk to Leaf about the situation. I know if I take care of this the 'hood way it's going to lead to more violence, and the truth is I don't want to take Snipa's life if I don't need to. Once Leaf walks into the room and gives me a dap I open up about it; "I got to holla at you, fam." Leaf already knows what it is about, but he lets me speak on what I am going through, "How you want to handle it, Crisis?" "I don't know what to do. I feel like Snipa tried to spare me at the party, but I think he has a direct order to take me out now"

Leaf kissed his teeth for at least five seconds before responding, "SK did too much, if he had just pulled out, they probably would've backed off and nothing would have happened." "I get that," I responded, "but it did happen, and I got to figure out how to get myself out of it." Leaf understood, "You trust me right, Crisis?" "Yeah of course, fam." I told him, then he continued, "If I let you hold a burner it's going to go left. Snipa can run up on you somewhere unexpected, you'll need to pull out, it'll be sloppy and it's a chance you'll go to jail for it if you're unprepared."

"This is not the Eastside anymore, you're a rising artist and a drug dealer. There is no other reason this kid is following you around other than the fact that he needs to prove that he can kill you. Unfortunately, he is going to keep coming back until you kill him. Here is what we're going to do; We are going to lure him and his boys somewhere, take him out and whoever he is

47

with, and then we slide back here safely. In the meantime, we're going to need to stash everything somewhere else."

I wasn't happy with the idea that Leaf presented to me, but I understood and accepted it was how it had to end. Snipa should have just left me alone, I wasn't bothering him at school, and I wasn't bothering him at the party. Just male bravado for no reason. If I don't do it to him, then he will do it to me. Let the best man win.

Me and Leaf went out to the bar to make some money, SK decided to go out of town for the time being, and Leaf let me hold onto his gun in the meantime. The night runs smoothly, and me and Leaf take a break to go outside and get some air. While outside, the moment arrives; We see the Durango. Leaf turns to me and tells me the play, "He's here, we're going to hop in the car and get this over with." I nod my head, and we took off. Leaf starts his car and by the first red light, we see the Durango take off driving.

We keep driving up until we leave the city limits, we stop on the side of the road somewhere deserted. The Durango pulls up right behind us, and the doors open. Shotta and Snipa step out. All four of us pull out our weapons, but still, nobody shoots. "We didn't even do anything, man!" I yelled at them, they don't respond. Pride mixed with guilt is a dangerous combination.

Shotta fires first and hits Leaf's Lexus, and I send a shot through the windshield of Snipa's Durango. Snipa gets enraged and shoots back at me, missing by an inch. In that moment, all four of us started to hear a siren in the distance. We lock our eyes and fire at each other one last time before getting back into our cars and rushing away. I really feel bad that Leaf got wrapped up in this, I don't think he's going to keep working with me if this is how week two is already going.

As we're driving off, I get apologetic with Leaf; "Fam, my bad about all of this for real. Any way I need to make up for this," before I could finish Leaf interrupt, "This is not your fault. You got to stop being so apologetic. These guys tried to rob you, they are trying to avenge somebody who you didn't even do anything to, and you're over here apologizing to me. This is just a day at the office. Do you think I can't handle the pressure or something? I accepted the risks when I got my first half-quarter, and you got to start accepting the terms and conditions, too. We are a team, and we're in this together."

"My goal is to push you to supreme being! You got to embrace your destiny, Crisis, this isn't the 'let's just play it safe and get by' crew, this is the 'go deep into the abyss' crew. You got to be able to manage the pain of not knowing when this is all going to stop. You got to be able to be ready to go wake up every day and be ready for whatever might go wrong. Why? So, you can be ready to take care of everything the right way."

These past few days showed me a lot, who's really got my back. Mimi has a completely new life in a new place, and could have anybody she wants in Florida, but she's choosing to show me the love she could be pouring into someone closer. Devon could have written me off the second I told him I was trapping, he got it and wants to keep me focused and motivated to pursue my real goals and ambitions. Leaf saw my potential and decided that all these problems were worth it so all of us could make it to the top one day. One thing I've learned from all this is to make sure I have the right group of friends around me

Chapter Five:
Home For the Holidays

Christmas break is coming up and things have been quiet. Snipa ended up transferring to a new school and his people have not been trying to find me or my people, they gave up. Leaf and Lacey finally got their own apartment downtown and I was able to stay with them, so we were out of the shelter. I saved up enough to get a new laptop, microphone, and recording software. I would be able to start working on music again soon. With everything going on I somehow managed to keep a C average, but best of all, Mimi might be coming home for the holidays!

My routine is still the same; Wake up go to school, come home, and then we make money. Leaf had me get a fake ID so I could get into more clubs and bars. He's been letting me practice driving his Lexus so I could get ready to get my driver's license next year. We started working at a nightclub downtown, and since I was moving up in the business, it was time to meet his plug, Paulie. Paulie was a mafioso man with a thick Italian accent, bald, and wouldn't wear anything other than Versace. Some people got an aura where you could just tell they are a killer before they even say anything to you, Paulie had that aura.

Going back home and claiming where I came from didn't even make sense to me anymore. I am turning sixteen in a couple of months, have my own place, and have money put away to buy a brand-new car. I knew exactly what I was going to get myself into: All-new Infiniti QE, four-door leather heated seats, electric engine, moon-roof, custom subwoofer, everything. Had I stayed at my aunt's house, I would have been stuck chasing my lifelong dream, without the resources to make it happen. Now I have what I need to succeed and be ready to go to the top when I turn eighteen.

Claiming Crip was starting to sound foolish too, I thought every single morning about that conversation with Mr. Hadi, and I thought about the situation everybody from the section was living in. We were all coming from poverty, but we were not really making much progress making it out of there. They were selling drugs to our neighbors, for cheap prices and insignificant amounts that they could afford. While doing that, we needed to worry about paying for protection (Knives, Guns, etc.) because enemies could come try to take our life at any moment. The code was that we could only rob our enemies, who were in the same situation, who also had limited resources.

It was a surrounding of low vibrational people engaging in activities that lowered our spirits further, and it was so normal to us that we never even thought to see it differently than "the way it is." I read a quote the other day, that said, "The tree does not stay beside the grass, even though they started from the same place; one elevated to a higher level," this resonated with me. Jay was in jail awaiting trial with no clue of when his trial date would even be. What would have happened if I went to hang out with him that day instead of Devon and Tay? One of my biggest goals with being successful in music was to take my family away from the Eastside, it is just a shame that I might make it in life, and they might not be there. I figured it was time to give my sister Tasha a call.

I went to her name in my phone and pressed call, but it went straight to voicemail, probably on sleep mode since it was late. I left a voicemail for her to hear when she could, "Hey fam, it's me. I know it's been a while, but I wanted to check in to see how you and Aunt Lala are doing and see if we could see a movie or go to the arcade or something soon. Just hit me back when you can. Love you sis." I ended the call and went to get some water. I still wasn't ready to drink alcohol, but I started smoking marijuana to help deal with everything I was going through.

Natasha Ibanez: *(9:18pm)*

Fam, I got kicked out too. I got into a relationship with a guy our aunt didn't like, and she told me to go live with him. I have not been reaching out either 'cause I have been in the same situation as you.

Me: *(9:18pm)*

Are you serious? How long has it been since you left?

Natasha Ibanez: *(9:20pm)*

About a month and a half, I have been staying with my boyfriend we are looking for a place. Where are you right now?

Me: *(9:22pm)*

I live on my friend's couch close to downtown, I am working two jobs and going to school still.

Natasha Ibanez: *(9:23pm)*

Thank God, I was wondering whether you were still in the shelter or not. Are you staying out of trouble?

Me: *(9:24pm)*

Not exactly. I can't really talk about it over the phone though. I am way safer now than I was before.

Natasha Ibanez: *(9:26pm)*

That is not good enough for me. I told you about getting involved with the wrong crowd. I told you what was going to happen to Jay, and I keep telling you what is going to happen to you if you don't break this generational curse.

Me: *(9:27pm)*

You know I didn't ask for this. I didn't ask for us to be forced to live in the Eastside. I didn't ask to be kicked out with zero resources or hope. I was left out in the cold to die, and all I am doing is refusing to die. I know you want better for me than this and I appreciate that, but this is all we have got right now. It is different than it was on the block. I promise you that all I am doing is getting money.

Natasha Ibanez: *(9:30pm)*

I get it. I really do get it Daniel, but you saw what happened to our dad, you saw what happened to our cousin, you have to understand why I didn't want this for you. There is another way, and I am always hard on you about this because I love you and I know how the story ends. If I didn't care, I would have always just let this happen. You are on a timer in life, there are things you can do to slow down the clock, and there are things you can do that are going to speed it up. But no matter what you do, one day that timer is going to run out. The decisions we make day by day determine when it is going to happen. If you really feel like you need to do this, you don't need to tell me what you are doing through the wire, but you need to tell me why you are doing it.

Me: *(9:35pm)*

I respect that. I am trying to buy a car, I am trying to get my own house, and I want to put money into music so I can make my money from that and that alone.

Natasha Ibanez: *(9:37pm)*

Talk to your friend, tell him we spoke and that you are going to be moving in with your sister. We need to stick together; it is a cold world out there and you need family. From the womb till the tomb we are all we got.

Me: *(9:40pm)*

I appreciate you sis. I have got to get ready for bed, it is a school night, can you meet me tomorrow?

Natasha Ibanez: *(9:42pm)*

Yes, for sure. Me and my boyfriend will pick you up from school, okay?

Me: *(9:42pm)*

Sounds good, can't wait. Goodnight fam.

I wasn't actually going to bed, but I knew there was no point explaining where I was off to. Me and Leaf had work to do, and I was going to mention the idea of moving in with my sister to him, but I was also going to need to explain to my sister that I work late nights now. Then another thought dawned on me that I hadn't considered; If Mimi comes back for Christmas, I am going to need to explain to her what it is I have been doing. It looks like December is going to be quite the rollercoaster.

Me and Leaf leave the apartment, and I open up when we get in the elevator, "Hey, I talked to my sister today, she was saying she wants us to get a two-bedroom apartment." Leaf got excited to hear that, "That's good little bro, you should take that offer." I was surprised, but relieved that this was his reaction. He continued, "You going back to Scarborough, or you think they want something downtown?" I responded, "I'm not sure yet, but would we still be rolling together to the club?" Leaf laughed, "It's up to you man, you know how to get here. If anything, if you go back to Scarborough, you can hold it down at the bar we used to work out of, gives me and Lacey some more space too."

Leaf was doing me a huge favor by putting me on and giving me the place to stay. I always wondered whether he was plain looking out for me or saw me as a business opportunity. However it might have started, it was clear to me now that Leaf

54

was someone who was really in my corner looking out for my best interest.

Something a lot of people need to understand when it comes to favors is you could repay someone just by accepting their help. What I mean by that is this; Not everybody is out to get you. Take me and Leaf, for example. Leaf helped me get on my feet, I gave him a loyal business partner that would never even think or consider turning on him. That was all he needed from me, and because I built a good reputation for myself as someone who is loyal, diligent, and ambitious, it was easy for Leaf to decide it was worth it to give me a chance. You have to build yourself and your character before people can help you.

We got to the club around 10pm, it was a high-end dress code club; Button-up shirts, no sports team hats, dress pants, sneakers were allowed, but you don't want to be that guy in there. I would go with the same type of outfit as I did when we were in Scarborough at the bar there and at the house party, just slightly changed. I got myself a black dress shirt, black dress pants, black wingtip dress shoes. I had a designer key pouch on me where I would keep my product, with a wallet and belt that matched, and because of Leaf and Paulies' connection with security, we were allowed to bring in anything necessary without trouble. The girls were beautiful, all in their twenties, all different races but the same types of outfits, straightened hair, plain and elegant hoop earrings, tennis chains and bracelets, designer purses, low skirts (even in December), and high heels. Some people would be happy to get paid to be surrounded by this, but for me that wasn't the case.

Leaf would always show up to the club with Lacey for a few reasons; first it gave them both time to spend together, second, she got to see for herself that he wasn't interested in any girls outside of her, finally, it ruined the possibility of any girl trying to get at him for a discount or free drugs. Since they were unaware of my age and the fact that my heart still belonged to somebody else (they wouldn't even care even if I did tell them about Mimi), I would catch the brunt of that problem. Being surrounded by that type of energy made me appreciate Mimi even more, and every single night I remember what people told me before she moved, that being young, I would find someone else. If I knew this was what else was out there, I would have given it even less thought, these women had no morals or character, half of them had on wedding/engagement rings letting other men grind on them and trying to seduce me into giving them free samples. There was one girl in particular, Vicky, who would always pressure me. She was more persistent than anybody I have ever met.

Vicky was a Filipino girl, twenty-five or twenty-six, perfectly straight and spotless white teeth, caked up face of mascara, deep pink lipstick that matched her eyelids, a sleeve tattoo on her left arm and another sleeve on her right leg. She was insanely beautiful, and I am not going to pretend she wasn't. Every regular male attendee at the club has tried to get her number before, except me and Leaf. Leaf she understood 'cause she was cool with Lacey, but for me she couldn't understand, which made me more attractive in her eyes. The way that I saw it, I was a challenge to her, and she needed to get with me to boost her ego. As I saw her walking up to me, I figured I should just tell her what is going on between me and Mimi tonight.

"Hey Big C!" That was her nickname for me, I never consented to it, but she was also my number one customer. She would always buy a couple of grams, and she would bring all her friends to buy a couple of grams. When guys would try to get with her and her homegirls, she would make them buy from me. Vicky was helping make sure I made at least one thousand dollars a night, and as much as I did appreciate that, I wasn't interested in letting anything happen with her beyond friendship. "What's good, Vick?" I replied, "Chilling like a villain you know me haha, how long you been here?" she asked. "About an hour, how you doing today?" I responded.

"Long day at the office, this guy at my job keeps trying to hit on me but he's so soft he doesn't want to come right out and say it, he'll just start random awkward conversations and it's like why are you doing this to yourself, you know?" The stalker girl at the club is telling me there is a stalker guy at her job, and we probably have all been in his situation before in one way or another. I decided to let her continue talking, and eventually when she asks how my day was, I can bring up Mimi.

"How about you, how was your day? What's new in the life of Crisis?" Vicki asked and I replied, "My day was good, my girlfriend's coming into town soon for Christmas so we're going to be able to catch up." Vicki looked shocked for the first five seconds of me delivering that news. She gathered herself mentally and started to enquire, "Woah wait, slow down, you have a girlfriend? What's her name? Why doesn't she live in the city? Why is this the first time you're mentioning her, mister?" I opened up to her, "Her name's Lakshmi, everybody calls her Mimi. She moved to Florida with her family a couple of months ago, and it's a complicated situation because of that, but, you know how it is when you have history with somebody right?" Vicky understood and respected it, now that she knows why I have been rejecting her advances.

"So that is why you never try to leave here with any girls. How old are you anyway? I know you're younger than me but, like, how old?" I lied about my age and told her, "We're both nineteen, but I knew her since I was about eleven or twelve." Vicky nodded, "yes that's a rare person to find. I respect why you want to be faithful to her, but as someone who has more experience, I got to be honest with you or I'm not helping you. Do you not think for a second, that she is also at a nightclub somewhere in Miami or wherever doing what you see me and my homegirls doing? You're a great guy, and I would hate to see you staying faithful to someone in another country and then in the end you get burnt, you know? If she is out having fun with guys, I don't think it would be so bad that you're over here having fun with girls."

I knew exactly what Vicky was trying to get me to do so I saw through it, I didn't want to explain to her how I knew. "I doubt it. If she did then she would be long gone by now, would she not?" I gave my honest and fair viewpoint on the situation, and she was ready to respond to anything I said to her. "I want to break this down for you from a woman's perspective, okay? If she didn't move, being the guy she knew from childhood, she knows she will need to have you around later on, for emotional support, a safety net, and a backup plan, but she's using you because at your age, there is not much more you can be for her. You're selling coke in a nightclub with a rap dream, she could be partying with rappers who have already made a million dollars from their craft right now.

Vicki continued, "Girls at nineteen, see the world as their playground. She's going to turn twenty in the new year, and she's going to want to spend that time enjoying herself. That means coming to places like this, dating other guys to know what else is out there, and just generally growing into a woman with her own identity. She won't be able to do that while worrying about you thousands of miles away, and if you make her do that, she's eventually going to start to resent you for making her miss out on life. I can tell you're serious and that you love her, and I'm sure that she docs feel the same way about you, too, but if she slips up out there, would you be able to forgive her?"

I knew what Vicki's intentions were, and I wasn't going to fall for it. Mimi isn't actually nineteen, so everything Vicki said wouldn't be relevant for another four years if that was even in Mimi's character. I am one hundred percent sure Mimi is a woman to die for and is in a school with thousands of other students, someone is trying to get the best of her every single day. If she let anything happen with anyone down there, I have to believe that she would be honest and tell me. I decided to gather my thoughts about the advice Vicki just gave me and figured it was best to ask Mimi myself what has been going on down south.

Me: *(11:11pm)*

Hey if you are still up, I need to talk to you.

Mimi Singh: *(11:11pm)*

11:11! Is everything okay babe?

Me: *(11:12pm)*

Not really. I am worried about us.

Mimi Singh: *(11:13pm)*

What's wrong? You know you can talk to me about anything, I am listening, and I will do my best to understand.

Me: *(11:15pm)*

Has there been a drift between us and am I holding you back from anything or anybody out in Orlando?

Mimi Singh: *(11:16pm)*

Daniel… you are making me anxious. What is this about? Did something happen?

Me: *(11:21pm)*

I am at work, and someone was telling me that I might be holding you back from experiencing life and now I am worried about everything. What if that email from Digital was my only chance to get a record deal? What if I can't graduate and keep my job? What if I never get stable enough to take care of you? What if I don't make it out of the street life? I love you so much and real love is selfless; I can't take away your youth waiting for me for it to end with me losing my life and I can't put you through that heartbreak. I don't know; I am confused.

Mimi Singh: *(11:26pm)*

I love you too, even though you are an idiot. Stop over-thinking. That is my choice to make if I want to wait for you. Its 2024, I don't need a man to take care of me, and even if I did what are you talking about? You are the most motivated person I have ever met, you have so many different talents there is no practical way for you to succeed in life. You have such incredible lyricism and I loved you long before you ever put anything out for the world to listen to. You have never failed a class in school before and you are one of the smartest people I know, I hear you talk, I see how you think, you really have nothing at all to worry about baby. I know you got a lot on your plate right now, and I know a lot of people would definitely fold if given your circumstances, but you have been pushing for over four months now on your own to make sure you still have a future, you can make it through any adversity and I am so proud and honored to even have known you let alone claim you. Everything is going to be okay, and I am right beside you in spirit every step of the way. Okay?

Mimi Singh: *(11:26pm)*

Never text me stupid shit like this again lol. You nerd <3

Me: *(11:29pm)*

I am speechless... You have no idea how badly I needed to read this babe. As long as you got me, I got you right back, just overwhelmed with everything going on you know.

Mimi Singh: *(11:30pm)*

And I totally get that, but just don't over think. If our souls are meant to find each other, they will, and no matter how far apart they may seem, they will always reconnect in the end. No pressure okay babe?

Me: *(11:30pm)*

Okay babe.

Mimi Singh: *(11:31pm)*

I am going to bed, some of us have school in the morning haha. Love you book <3.

Me: *(11:31pm)*

Goodnight gorgeous, sweet dreams and take care I love you too <3.

That was the Mimi I knew and loved. Mimi was always my biggest support, and I knew I needed her more than I needed anything or anyone else. Things could be at their absolute bleakest for me, and when there is no reason to find a purpose, I always have her. I don't know if she will ever truly realize how much I love her, but I know no matter what happens, I had the privilege to experience true love on earth. That is something I will always be grateful for no matter what. Girls like Mimi deserve nothing but the best.

The next day was the last day of school before the Christmas break, we were having a party in Mr. Hadi's class. Board games, pizza, and pop-- classic last day of school activities. Our final assignment was going to be assigned on our first day back from the holidays, and we got our last test results back yesterday. I had worked my way up to a 92.5 average in his class, I had a seventy-eight in Ms. Caruso's class, and my other two classes I really didn't care about and was at about a sixty-five for both, I was passing all of the tests, and that was all I needed right now. Too much was happening in my personal life to prioritize everything.

After Mr. Hadi's class, I decided to text my sister and get permission to leave school early. We needed to find the apartment, and not only that, I was going to see Mimi for the first time since August this weekend. I was nervous as much as I was excited, if you're not nervous for a big date, then you don't care about the person as much as you think you do.

I got everything out of my locker and into my bag, then I headed out of the building. I start to get an eerie feeling as soon as I open the door. I can hear a drill song blasting from a car somewhere, unsure if it is coming from the street, the parking lot, or even the plaza down the street. I start walking through the parking lot to the bus, and the music starts to get louder. Before I know it, I see Snipa's Durango, with him, Shotta, and two other guys in red bandanas covering their face, aiming their weapons in mine. Shotta always had a double barrel shotgun with him, Snipa would always carry a desert eagle on him, and the two guys in the back were both carrying revolvers. "Don't think for a second we forgot about you!" Shotta exclaimed.

I was at school and couldn't have a weapon on me, all of them knew that. I didn't shoot anybody, I didn't instigate anything, and these guys will not let up and let me live. The fact that Leaf said I'm going to need to kill Snipa and Shotta, when he heavily disagreed with gang politics really spoke volumes. I am really starting to see how he was right. My plans for the day were to meet my sister and her boyfriend then find an apartment. Now, I am starting to get sick of this.

"Look, if you are going to shoot, just go ahead and do it. I didn't do anything to Fredo! I am right here." I shouted at them, one thing I am not going to do is live my life looking over my shoulder. If I die right now, then I die right now. If I don't, then Snipa is going to wish that he took me out right now anyway. Snipa pointed and laughed, pressed the trigger, and POW! I looked at my parka, there was a hole at the top of the left sleeve. I turned my head to see them driving off. I start to panic and remove my jacket to see the wound, thankfully it just ripped through the jacket, only slightly grazing my skin.

I took a minute to sit down and collect myself, then kept waiting for the bus. My blood was boiling, I kept trying to avoid them so I could just focus on money and music, but clearly, they're not going to let me do that. It's becoming clear, I am going to need to take out Snipa and Shotta. The sooner I do it, the better. I put on some music after I put my parka back on, and I keep waiting for the bus. They might think they have won for now, but payback is coming.

I went to the mall to meet my sister and her boyfriend, his name was Antoine. He was light skin, about six-feet tall, wearing a black parka with a baseball cap on. He's on his laptop looking at a website showing what apartments are available to rent. Natasha had them narrowed down to four options. All they wanted to know was which out of the four remaining options suited me best. One was $1200 for two-bedrooms, one was $1300 for a bedroom and a den, one was $1000 for a one-bedroom, and I would need to sleep in the living room, and the last one was $1100 for a two bedroom, but in an area that didn't have many bus routes. My vote was the final one.

We called the number on the ad and drove over at once. Antoine had an all blacked out Beamer, limo tint windows, black rims, and blacked out rear lights. We got there and saw it in person, it looked way better than the ad. The closest bus was about 20 minutes from the apartment, but it went directly to my school. Both rooms were spacious, and we would be able to move in the same day. Since it was so close to the new year the landlord decided to give us it early. We paid first and last month's rent, and Natasha and Antoine called the moving company to get started with bringing their things there.

I had to go back to Leaf's apartment to pick up my clothes and laptop. I still had a reference from the shelter for a furniture bank to get a bed, desk, and dresser to fill my new room. This was going to be the first time in my life I had my own bedroom; I always had to share with Jay or Natasha before, then Leaf, and now I had one all to myself, just in time for Mimi's return.

When I got to the furniture bank, I saw a beige-wood bed frame that could fit a California King sized mattress, a vanity mirror with a dresser underneath, and a desk, all in the same color that would match in my new room. I had to put a sticker on all three and then choose a mattress for the bed. There was a memory foam California king mattress available that would fit perfectly on the frame, so I picked that one, and got on the bus toward Leaf's.

I had everything set up at my new place by the following afternoon, and I was waiting for a text from Mimi to let me know she was on her way to the airport. I shaved, had an appointment to get a haircut, and had just got a new bottle of the cologne I always wore. I had money for two taxis, dinner at a nice restaurant, and then a movie afterwards. I knew what Mimi's parent's rules were, so I had to be respectful and make sure she is home by 9pm. If I got her in trouble, it would be a wrap.

It was Saturday morning, and one of the most important days of my adolescence thus far. I have to get ready and meet Mimi for our date, I look outside of my new apartment windows and see the pale grey sky, with pebble-sized snowflakes falling like leaves falling from a tree. It was peaceful, a fresh layer of snow is settled onto the ground; Enough that the Town Centre will not be crowded, but not too much that we would get stuck. I was optimistic about today, but nervous I'd be awkward after four months apart. With no time to overthink, I start to get ready.

When the weather gets like this, dressing up is easy; I stitched up my parka from where the bullet went through, then can match it with a toque, cargo pants and snow boots. The new apartment had sliding mirrors for closet doors, so as I got everything together, I looked at myself and saw a reflection of a lot of things. I was proud of the man who I was becoming, I was given every reason to drop out of school and quit making music, and I stayed. I could have let the drug dealer lifestyle alienate me from people like Mimi and Devon, and I didn't. I could have flushed my real job down the toilet and quit on my community, and I didn't. I was growing to be a man of high moral standards, fiercely loyal, true to where I came from, and found my true nature in the face of adversity.

I headed downstairs and got on the bus, I put my face mask on and hood up to keep warm. I stared into the distance and started visualizing how I want today to go. I remembered Mimi's favorite restaurant at the food court was the Hakka restaurant, and being a Scorpio, she always had a fondness for scary movies. The plan was simple, meet at the subway station, spend the day at the mall, lunch, a movie, and take a taxi with her back home in time for her curfew. I can do this.

The bus brought me to the subway station, I texted her to let her know I was there and went to the food stand. I got a Jamaican beef patty, a coconut water, along with a pack of spearmint gum. I finish eating my patty and see her bus pull into the station, I walk over to see if she will come out, and I see her walking out of the back door. We locked eyes as her feet touched the ground and a warm feeling entered my spirit, it really was as if not a day had passed since we were by the water over the summer. Mimi ran into my arms and started squeezing me tightly in a hug, slowly but surely continuing to tighten her grip with no intention of letting go, the hug lasted at least five minutes before we moved our faces back, looked into each other's eyes again, and kissed for the first time since she moved to Florida.

"I missed you so much, Daniel!" Mimi exclaimed while maintaining a vice grip around me. "I missed you too Meems, I've been thinking of this moment every day since you left," I replied. "No way, really? So, none of these Toronto girls could take you away, huh?" Mimi joked playfully, and I made it clear, "You know none of them could ever stand a chance," and her face was glowing with happiness. I was so happy I didn't listen to Vicki, seeing Mimi in person and refusing to settle for anyone other than her was absolutely the right decision. We got on the bus to the mall and started our date.

The first place we went to was the shoe store, I had a passion for Air Jordan's, and Mimi had the same passion for Nikes. I picked up the Air Max 90's, they were all black with an orange sole. I showed them to Mimi and told her, "You could rock these any day" and she looked at them in awe. I asked the nearest associate to get a pair in her size and to ring it up. We went to the cashier, and I took out three-hundred dollars cash, all in one-hundred-dollar bills. Mimi gave me a light backhanded slap to the shoulder and whispered to me "put that away you're going to make yourself a target!"

"You're right, my bad" I corrected myself and folded them back up. The cashier put in the total and asked me to pay, "Your total comes out to one-hundred and ninety-two dollars and ten cents," I handed her two of the hundred-dollar bills that were in my pocket, got my change then carried the shoes for Mimi. "I am grateful babe, thank you so much and sorry for doing that, but I just want you to be careful. I won't always be here to protect you haha" Mimi explained jokingly, and we both started laughing, "you're right. That's my girl, Mrs. Right." Mimi couldn't stop smiling after hearing that until we got to the food court. We got to Hakka and placed our order; Large Chili Tofu on veggie fried rice, and we found a place to sit and eat.

I took her jacket for her and opened the food container so we could share it, then Mimi threw me off with a question I hoped wouldn't be asked, "So are you planning on telling me what happened to your jacket?" She saw the stitched-up hole, and I had no intentions of lying to her about what has been going on in her absence, but I didn't want to ruin the mood. "It's a long story, I'll tell you later, okay?" Mimi nodded and let me sit down before continuing, "I can kind of piece it together myself, a fifteen-year-old runaway working at a nightclub with a thousand dollars handy for a mall-date, who was just living with active Crip members before I moved away. You're selling drugs and I know, and I'm not mad at you. I get why you are doing it, but I don't want anything happening to you. If I woke up over a thousand miles away, and had to find out through Devon or Natasha that something happened to you, how do you think that would make me feel? If we're still making this work it's not just you out there, you're not alone like you think you are."

We started eating and I started explaining my side of things, "You're right, and this is not something I'm going to be doing forever, I'm already out of it. Me and Natasha just got an apartment, I got enough stashed up to buy a car when I get my license, I got a studio setup, I just need to keep building enough so I can make money legally. My jacket had nothing to do with this. You remember Jason, right? It was because of those guys. I know this is hard for you Mimi, but you got to understand how this is hard for me too. This is temporary. I can't promise that I'll be out by the next time you see, but I can promise that I am doing everything in my power to get out before it is too late."

Mimi was looking down at the food, and I could see the thoughts processing through her mind. As she was almost done eating, she started nodding. She took a deep breath in, looked up at me and then continue, "I get it, Daniel, you got to do what it takes to survive. If there is any way I can help you out, I have your back. I want to see you make it out of this. I need to see you make it out of this, and I know you well enough to know you are smart enough to do just that."

Mimi reached across the table and put her right hand in mine, then intertwined her fingers with mine, her thumb underneath my thumb. She instructed me to close my eyes, "Even though I walk through the valley of the shadow of death, I will fear no evil, for God you are with me, your rod, and your staff, they comfort me. You provide a table before me in the presence of my enemies, you anoint my head with oil, my cup overflows. Surely your goodness and love will follow me all the days of my life, and I will dwell in the house of the Lord, forever. Amen," she prayed.

67

We both opened our eyes and looked at each other, rejuvenated. I felt my phone vibrate in my pocket, but I knew it wasn't the time to check it; it had to wait. I got up from the table, still holding Mimis hand, and helped her stand up from the table, we gave each other another long hug. I felt my phone vibrating again, and so did Mimi. Instead of reaching for my phone, I took out two sticks of gum, taking one for myself and giving one to Mimi. It was time to see what movies were playing today.

We saw the movie options as we walked into the theatre, and none of them seemed interesting. I decided to just bring her to the arcade in the theatre. We started off playing a shooting game where zombies were attacking us. I joked to her saying, "show me what the open-carry state's about." She giggled and got ready to aim. After a while we switched to a street racing game, she picked the Mitsubishi Lancer, and I picked the Nissan Skyline. Next, we played the basketball free throw game, final score was 119-120, Mimi. I could have won if my phone stopped vibrating, I know it's serious at this point, but I still need to wait.

Mimi goes to the bathroom, and I finally check my phone while I wait for her. I have fifteen missed calls from Leaf, along with a text message telling me I need to call him back and meet him tonight. I got an eerie feeling, I was shaking inside. I could feel something in my throat drop all the way down into my stomach. Something had to be very wrong for him to call me this early in the day like this, along with the text message to meet him without context. Whatever it is, if I text him right now, something tells me he will not even want to respond through a text message. I must be grateful for the day I had, because it's not going to be a good night.

Mimi comes back from the washroom, and we walk around the mall for a little longer. It was getting close to dinner time, and it was best to let her have dinner with her family, then I could see what Leaf had to talk about. I got her a chocolate bar from the theatre and then we started walking back to the bus. Insecurity got the best of me though, and I had to ask her.

"Did today go, okay?" She laughed and responded, "of course it did, Daniel, you're a good guy, you really need to give yourself more credit. We did everything I wanted to do today." I felt relieved and continued, "I'm glad I could do that for you. Think we'll have time to do this again before you head back south?" Mimi kissed me, deeper than she ever had before, and told me "Maybe, but just in case I had to give you that."

We got off the bus and went our separate ways, Mimi went to her house, and as I was going to wait for my bus. I knew it was time to call Leaf. It rang one time and I instantly heard, "Where the hell you been all day, man? You gotta come to Scarborough General Hospital right now." My heart dropped and I asked, "what happened, Leaf?" "Get here A.S.A.P. and head to room 504." I get on a different bus and go to the hospital. I went to the room, I am ending the best day in the worst way possible.

There's a police officer outside of the hospital room, middle-aged, white, overweight, with a bald spot similar to Paulie's. Had I not known any better, I would have thought it was Paulie. No sunglasses today, however, and his eyes were very bloodshot, as if he had been pulling a double shift and just saw something very traumatic. I am never going to feel that type of empathy for a constable though; if we don't get sympathy as the people living through what it is they are seeing us go through, why should anyone care? Us putting the bandana in our back pocket, is the same as them putting the badge on their chest.

The officer stopped me before going in, putting his hand against my shoulder before asking me, "What's your relationship to the victim?" I told him in an exhausted voice from running from the bus to the building, "I'm a friend of the family. I was told to get here as soon as I could." The police officer looked at me and said "Alright, well, if his mom says it's okay, you can come in." Just as he opens the door, I hear a very deep, Caribbean accent screaming and crying. "I moved all the way to Toronto, sacrificed everything I had, worked myself to the bone every single day, *overtime*, so that my son would NEVER have to experience this. I MUST KNOW who did this to my son."

I walk into the room, and there was SK's mom yelling at another police officer in the room. That's when it clicked, SK got shot. Leaf and Lacey were also in the room. I locked eyes with Leaf, we both knew who did it, and we both knew what time it was. I looked down at S.K., he was in a coma and had a ventilator over his face, a blanket covering the rest of his body. The doctor's assessment was that he suffered five gunshot wounds: one to his chest, one to his shoulder, one to his left forearm, one to his pelvis, missing his spine by an inch and a half, and one to his right leg. Fortunately, no major organs were hit, and he was expected to make a full recovery after a few months of rehabilitation.

Unfortunately, me and SK had been fired at by the same people in the span of a week. Snipa and Shotty realized they missed me after there was no reports of a shooting, and they went to get their "revenge" through somebody else. If what happened at the bus stop wasn't the final straw, this was. Now that Leaf is even down for the mission, it really is about to be over. Me and Leaf went out for a smoke, we are going to plan this out properly.

Leaf pulled out his cigarette and was speaking as he was smoking, "This is ending tonight, you know that right? I told you we should never have gone to that party, but that doesn't matter now. I'm not into this beef, this is horrible for business, but if war brings peace, I'm with it. SK's mom is right, she didn't move here for this, my family didn't move here for this, and your family didn't move here for this, shit, not even Snipa and Shotty's families moved here for this. This has gone too far, and I know exactly where they at."

70

Leaf continued before outing his cigarette, "Lacey got a homegirl who knows somebody from their side. There's going to be a party at a bar just outside town, and they're already there. We can put the work in on them from outside the bar, flee the scene. Nobody there knows where I live, where you live, and they are def not going to know where SK lives. We get them out of the picture, nobody else has a motive to come for us. We were their opportunity to prove themselves, and they couldn't. I promise you, you got nothing to worry about."

Me and Leaf shook hands and drove out. Leaf went to the suburb just outside of town that I thought was going to be where the party was, but not yet. Leaf drove us to a white van, which was rented out before he went to the hospital. Leaf was never going to do anything that could potentially go wrong and only made calculated moves. From there we drove twenty minutes further away from Toronto, and then pulled into a mini plaza that had Snipa's Durango parked outside.

We drove past the bar very slowly and saw both Snipa and Shotty drinking. They were intoxicated and would eventually come outside to smoke. Leaf handed me his pistol with a silencer attached. It could go one of two ways; They come outside to smoke, and we take them out and leave without even going inside, or we catch them in the washroom and walk out. The cameras inside would make the second one a higher risk. It was smartest to stay parked in the lot and wait for them to come outside.

We waited in the car for about an hour. I really didn't want to do this, everything I've done since I was kicked out were things I really didn't want to do, too. This was the moment I've worried about since the party happened, but if this didn't happen today, they would come after me again. It wasn't anything personal, there was no malice, but I knew I was going to do what needed to be done. It comes down to me or them, and I have no choice but to pick them.

Finally, Shotty comes out and Snipa follows him, and they went to the alleyway beside the plaza, away from the cameras. It was go-time, me and Leaf ran out of the van and rushed to the alley. We pulled out our weapons and both Snipa and Shotta put their hands up. Leaf instantly shot Shotta in the shoulder, the impact from the bullet knocking him to the ground. While Shotta was falling, Leaf emptied the clip on him, releasing sixteen more bullets before Shotta could land on the ground. He gasped one last time, you could feel life leaving his body. It was over.

Snipa screamed while looking at Shotty, He tried to play innocent. "You guys win, you feel good now, Crisis? You're going to shoot somebody you knew your whole life? That make you feel like a man?" Enraged, I tell him, "You been trying to shoot me for months, and if you just left me alone, it would never have come to this. I am done making excuses to keep you alive." Snipa continues trying to talk me out of it while reaching for the ground, "No I didn't I was just joking, I'm telling you, just, just." Snipa picked up a chunk of ice from the ground and threw it right at me, I kicked it. The ice hit his right shin, instantly bringing him to the ground.

I stood over him and pointed the silenced pistol at his head. "You got something left to say to me?" I asked Snipa. He knew it was over, he responded, "Yeah, I do. You're a wasteman and you are never going to make it." I breathed in, and said my final words to him, "Should've left me alone fam." I pulled the trigger and it was finally over. The only thing left to do was get away from the scene before anybody noticed.

I felt numb after shooting Jason. As we were fleeing the scene, I was looking out of the window coming to terms with what just happened. My vision was black and white as I observed the scenery around me, then, I had a flashback. One time, me and Jason were on the track at our elementary school during recess, in third grade. We were throwing tennis balls at each other, making jokes, and laughing together as children.

Another flashback came, this time around grade six. Someone in the eighth grade tried to pick on me, Jason, Taylor, and Devon so we stole his basketball, I would pass it to Jason, then when he got close to Jason, Jason would pass it to Taylor, then to Devon then back to me. All four of us got called down to the principal's office, and we all had each other's backs. We got there, and the eighth grader was crying. This made Jason laugh the exact same way he did when he shot at me, which brought me to another memory.

The last flashback came from the beginning of grade eight, I had a brand-new Toronto Blue Jays fitted from the summer. We were all in line waiting to go into class, and he sprayed a canned body spray into the hat, so that I needed to throw it out. Then I remembered him spitting on my chair a month later, then I remembered everything that happened since we started high school. After those thoughts started making their way in, the color in my vision returned, I started to make peace with the situation. Once I accepted that I had no choice, I was hurt and disappointed, but I had accepted the situation.

Me and Leaf didn't say a word to each other the entire drive. Neither of us were happy about it, but we put it off as long as we could; It was necessary. We got back to Leaf's Lexus, and afterwards, set the white van on fire. Leaf broke the silence once he started his car, "If I were you, Crisis, I would take the rest of the year off from work. It's fine, talk to Mimi, talk to your aunt, you want to make amends where you can."

"My aunt has my phone number; I haven't changed it." I replied, still holding a grudge for her kicking me out. Leaf rolled his eyes and continued, "You don't think she knows that she was wrong? Look what we just had to do, we live in a fucked-up city, in a fucked-up world. You can make it right with anybody. Believe that.

You have a chip on your shoulder about your family, Snipa also has a chip on his shoulder about his family, and y'all needed someone else to take it out on cause y'all can't take it out on the real source. When you learn to let go of these things gracefully, that's when you can get blessings and get money, which gives you legitimate power to make changes in our community. All that crab-bucket mentality does is force everybody to stay broke. Pointless, low vibrational, bottom feeder behavior."

Leaf dropped me off at my apartment, shook my hand, and told me one last thing, "this was your last year of being in these problems, come the new year, I promised you a million. We are going to get that, and we're going to make it out of this." I agreed and got out of the car. A soon as I closed the door, he drove back towards the hospital. I went upstairs, and thought about calling my aunt Lala, but I wasn't ready. I needed to tell someone else I got home safely.

Me: *(6:05pm)*

Hey there is an emergency, I hope you got home okay, but I got to check into something.

Mimi Singh: *(6:20pm)*

Just walking in the house now, are you safe??

Mimi Singh: *(8:00pm)*

For God's sake Crisis. I will just take that as a no.

Mimi Singh: *(8:30pm)*

Can you please not do this right after I spent a day with you? I just told you how hard this stuff is on me hours ago.

Me: *(9:05pm)*

I couldn't text back until now, I am sorry. I get why you are worried, and I am sorry for not responding sooner. I am safe, me and Jay's friend got shot so I had to see him and his mom in the hospital. He is going to be okay and recover but I still had to go and check in on him.

Mimi Singh: *(9:10pm)*

It was Jason, wasn't it? Do you know how much I just cried thinking something happened to you?

Me: *(9:11pm)*

That is not confirmed, and you know I can't go into details about stuff like this over the phone.

Mimi Singh: *(9:11pm)*

Well, something else is confirmed about him.

Me: *(9:12pm)*

Mimi, what are you saying?

Mimi Singh: *(9:13pm)*

You can't talk about it over the phone. You need to promise me it will never happen again.

Me: *(9:14pm)*

I really had no choice, but you have my word, I am out of the Eastside.

Mimi Singh: *(9:15pm)*

Night.

Chapter Six:
Canadian Winter

It's the new year in Toronto, the weather is -15° Celsius, and the ground is covered in snow and ice. Most people are hibernating, giving themselves a break after partying all night last night. I decided it was best to just stay inside and lay low and see what options I have available to make money outside of the city. Leaf wanted to meet up with Paulie to ask about taking a shipment from Montreal back to Toronto. Leaf was moving up in the game, and me being his protégé, that meant I was as well.

I called Mimi a couple of times, but since she got back to Orlando, she hasn't been returning any of my calls. Natasha told me to give her space, and I understand she's upset with me about what happened after our date. It was something I couldn't get my mind off and was heartbreaking for me on both levels. Not only did I have to live with Jason's blood on my hands, but I also had to live with the fact that I might have lost Mimi in the crossfire. I was torn and confused; I had to look in the mirror to tell myself the same thing I told myself when she first moved. *Real love is releasable; If two souls are meant to find each other, they will, and no matter how far apart they may seem, they will always reconnect in the end.*

Leaf gave me a call while I was watching TV with Natasha and Antoine, "Hey, business meeting, meet me in the parking lot." I gave Antoine a handshake and Natasha a hug, then walked to the elevator. I was expecting to see Leaf's Lexus when I got outside of the lobby, however, I saw a new car Leaf

76

and Paulie in a new car. It was a black Rolls-Royce Ghost sedan with a silver hood, roof, and trunk, with off-white seats and stars on the roof inside. I got in the back seat and shook both of their hands, Paulie got started talking business.

"So, I have known Leaf for a long time, and I know he speaks highly of you. You are someone he shows me I can trust, because I trust him. Where I'm going with this is, I got something that belongs to me coming in from back home and yous guys are the people I trust to deliver it to me. Canada is a big, big country, but it is also really small. Toronto has a lake that shares a border with America, which is good for guns. That's what they're dropping off. Montreal has a port, where we can bring in drugs from anywhere on the Atlantic Ocean, which is what America is looking for, you see where I'm going with this?

So, what I need you two to do for me, is pick up my package in Montreal, bring it back here to me, and I'll take it from there. Half of it is going to stay with me and I will end up giving part of it to yous guys. The rest of it is going to the other side of that lake, capisce?" Leaf and I nodded in agreement. "Alright, so this is the address, 5555 St. Catherine Street, you don't put this into the GPS, you put this hotel across the street into your GPS. Spend the night over there, then come back the next morning with the stuff."

Paulie drove me and Leaf back to Leaf's Lexus at the Town Centre parking lot. He and I started getting ready for the trip. When it's your first time doing something new, naturally, you'll feel nervous. When you remember you just killed two enemy gang members, you realize you are better off spending time away from the city where it happened. So, the first thing to decide was what to eat for lunch before hitting the road. The hotel was about six hours away from us, so we were going to need some food and some gas before heading out there.

We got some burgers and some gas then headed straight onto the highway. The highway during the winter is usually haphazard; It could be the safest road or the most dangerous road. Since the snowstorm occurred yesterday, they have already had a chance to plow and salt it, making it safe for a long trip. There was higher than average traffic, so many people came into the city to celebrate New Year's Eve, so that was inevitable. By the time we were about an hour away from the city, the rest of the roads were clear.

Leaf started playing instrumentals from his phone through the car's Bluetooth, and asked me, "When are you going to start putting out music again? Tell me this beat's not lit! We got a long drive ahead, don't forget why I put you on in the first place." I started nodding my head to the beat, I was feeling it. It was a faster sounding beat, but it had pain behind it. The main melody was a piano playing minor chords, with an 808 bassline and a drill-style drum pattern behind it. My mind was taking me everywhere; My aunt kicking me out, skipping rocks by the water with Mimi, and then it brought me to a different place. Seeing Fredo die, seeing Brandon and Jason die, and then seeing Jay get arrested.

Once it reached the hook, a trumpet sample came into it with an element of sadness, but it made it triumphant. I knew this was the beat I needed to hear, I didn't even realize I had fallen out of love with music, but this made me fall right back in love with it. Being in survival mode, making money from the streets, it made it easy for me to forget why I took to music to begin with. I realized after I bought the microphone, midi board, and the laptop, I never actually made anything. Chasing money makes it easy to lose focus on every single thing other than money, and sometimes, you don't realize it until it is too late. This is why you have to stick to the right people who want to see you win.

"Yeah fam, send me this beat. I got something deep for it, but it's going to have to wait till we're back in Scarborough." I told Leaf and he agreed, "Crisis, give this one year, remember where I met you. We didn't meet by accident, and we didn't come this far just to come this far. We need a way out of the game eventually, and this is going to be your way out. I have to make sure me and Lacey can buy a house one day. I want to make sure you and that girl Mimi can buy a house one day. Remember what I showed you, the system is designed for us to fail, it's on *us* to beat the system. Show our kids that the way we had to survive was bull-shit and make sure they have better options than we did. *That's* what this is all about."

After that speech, I was pumped up and ready to handle business. I had my goals down pat, I had people around me who with goals that will make sure we can work together and make anything happen. The only thing to do is enjoy the ride to Montreal and focus on the road to the good life. Once we were more than halfway through, it was time to fill up the car and get some food again. The station we stopped at was huge because it was far from any big city, they had to make sure it had everything; There was a burger spot, a fried chicken spot, even a taco spot, plus a convenience store.

Leaf went to get some chicken, and I wanted to get a burrito. We both had burgers last time we ate so neither of us wanted to eat the same meal twice. I went to the convenience store to get a fruit punch, and then we went to sit down to eat. I did the sign of the cross, thanked God for the food, opportunity, and for forgiveness and protection. There's a lot on the table, but I need things to go right. I learned it's important to always keep your morals no matter what it is you are doing.

We finished eating and got back on the highway. GPS said we were only two and a half hours away, it should go by fast. In the meantime, I wanted to hear more instrumentals and think about things to write. The countryside was beautiful, and it cleared my mind a lot just looking out from the highway at the tall, long array of trees. When you have only lived in one place your entire life and start realizing how big the world around you actually is, it makes it a lot easier to want more out of life. I was excited for this new year of my life; I could feel that I was so close to the breakthrough.

We could see a flag waving in the distance. It was royal blue with a white cross going through the middle, and the fleur-de-lis in each corner. It was attached to a big road sign that was slowing becoming more legible. The first word I could read said *"Bienvenue,"* as we got closer to the sign, it read in different languages. On the top it said, *"Welcome,"* underneath, *"welta'sualuleg"* and then, at the bottom as we drove passed, I could read *"Quebec."* We have crossed the border and are officially in another province. GPS said we were about an hour away from the Hotel, and I was excited to see what this new place was going to be like.

We eventually crossed a bridge and entered the city limits; I never even knew Montreal was an island until today. All the buildings were older architectural structures, all of them covered with graffiti. Not just regular graffiti like what I was used to seeing in Scarborough, every tag had multiple colors, had faces and characters, and you could tell that they were allowed to take their time and make something beautiful. It was celebrated here as art and even encouraged. All the restaurants and businesses had French names, even ones you would see in Toronto had a French name change. We drove past a KFC with the image of the Colonel Sanders and everything, only the acronym attached read *PFK*. It really felt like we stepped into a completely different country, even the air and energy was different than Toronto.

We arrived at the hotel, and it was by far the nicest building I had ever seen. We got to the valet zone and saw a huge lobby through a giant revolving door entrance and renaissance style tiling in the parking foyer. We walked in and the first thing I saw was the walls covered by an artificial fireplace, dimmed lighting, a black marble floor and a long line at the front desk. We went in and Leaf gave them the information for our reservation. We got the key card and made our way up to our room.

80

We saw the room and it was bigger than my aunt's entire home. It was two beds in different rooms, both rooms had a California king sized bed and a fifty-inch screen TV. The sheets were all white and looked brand new, as if they had never been used. The washroom had a bathtub that looked like it was a jacuzzi, two different sinks, and a mirror that covered the entire wall sitting behind the counter. This was unlike anything I have ever seen, experienced, or even fathomed before.

We put our bags down and got ready for the meetup. There was an Italian restaurant down the street, Santo Marco, where we were supposed to pick up our package. Leaf turned to me quick and asked me, "You ready to change your life today, C?" I nodded, told him "Yeah, man," gave him a dap and we brought it in and headed back downstairs. As the elevator doors closed, Leaf told me, "Let me do all the talking, and you just carry it back up here, got it?" I nodded again and we walked outside.

We get to Santo Marco and there was an older Italian lady behind the register. She sees me and Leaf walking up to her, she looks as if she's been expecting us. Leaf breaks the ice, "We called in a couple hours ago for pickup, is our order prepared?" The host responds in a thick Italian accent, "Right in time, this was taking up too much space in the kitchen, we have more orders to fill, huh?" She walks into the kitchen and pulls out a huge brown paper bag with the Santo Marco logo on it and puts it on the counter.

I went to pick it up, and it was surprisingly lighter than I expected, less than 10 pounds total. We got back to our hotel suite and looked at in the bag. There was one empty container for us to use on the scale for measuring, then about three other containers full of cocaine. Leaf confirmed it was the right amount, and we put them all back in the paper bag and put it in the minifridge in our suite. Leaf was ecstatic, like he waited his whole life for this moment, he turned to me and said, "We got to go out to celebrate this C, we bout to run Scarborough when we get home!" I wanted to party, but I had some other things on my mind. I told him, "If you want to see the town that's cool, but I'm going to stay here and keep an eye on things." Leaf respected it and shrugged, "that's cool man." He shook my hand and headed out the door.

The first thing I did was put on the piano beat Leaf was playing on the way here. I wanted to start writing, but as I looked in the notes on my phone, nothing was really coming to me. I knew whatever I said on this beat was going to make it one of the most important songs I will ever write. It just wasn't the right time to start. It was about 8pm, and Mimi was still on my mind. For some reason I kept wishing I could hear from her, and if she would listen to me, give me another chance.

Mimi Singh: *(8:08pm)*

Hey, so sorry I have been distant. I dropped my phone the same night we met, and I just got it fixed today. I feel like you are mad at me, but I am sorry about the distance.

Me: *(8:09pm)*

Mimi! I have been trying to call you since that day. I thought you were not answering because you were mad at me. Are you okay?

Mimi Singh: *(8:10pm)*

Yeah, I am doing good just getting ready for school next week. How is the new place and your sister been?

Me: *(8:11pm)*

Are we okay? I am actually out of town right now, going back tomorrow though.

Mimi Singh: *(8:12pm)*

Oh, where did you go? And yes Daniel, I just want better for you. I remember you being someone so full of potential with so many options so seeing you live dangerously is hard for me to process and you need to be able to understand that.

Me: *(8:13pm)*

I get that, I want better for me too. I am in Montreal with one of my homies, he is good people next time you come to visit we should all get together, he wants me to get back to music too. Its been a lot of changes in life over the passed few months I had to adapt to, this is just the present, it will not be the future.

Mimi Singh: *(8:14pm)*

I appreciate that a lot, I love you Daniel, I am really grateful we got to talk. I am back in March, okay?

Me: *(8:15pm)*

I love you too and I can't wait to see you again. I got to take care of business, but I am grateful we got to talk too.

Mimi Singh: *(8:16pm)*

Okay babe be careful.

I spent the rest of the night relaxing and enjoying the hotel amenities. I looked out at the Montreal Skyline before going to bed early. I knew I made the right decision to stay inside, and I got big plans for when I get back into the city tomorrow. I woke up early to sounds of moaning and vomiting, I got out of bed and saw Leaf in the bathroom, hungover like I had never seen before. I packed the drugs in my backpack and tried to give him the complimentary tea and water to help get him good. There was no way Leaf of all people would let something like this happen on such a crucial day, so I was annoyed, but I let it go, we got to figure out our way back to town.

"Are you good to drive?" I asked Leaf, and he didn't even try to defend that he is. He holds his keys up to me and responds, "Nope, I'm not, this is really your big weekend, Crisis." This man wants me to drive his car for six hours across a provincial border, with three kilograms of cocaine in the backseat. I don't even have a license, I'm underage. I can't believe this is happening, but I take the keys anyway. I drag Leaf downstairs to checkout, and I get behind the wheel.

I turn to Leaf, leaning back looking like he was about to die in the passenger seat, and reaffirm this is the right decision, "Fam, are you sure I can handle this?" Leaf responds, "Listen, if you can pull this off there is no way you won't get your driver's license when you turn sixteen. Focus on the destination, not the journey my friend." I roll my eyes, shake my head, and get on the road. I was nervous for the first few streets, then once I got on the highway, it was like all my fears were gone.

We drove through the city, passed the Quebec-Ontario border and I started to feel hungry, realizing food will help bring Leaf back to life too. I turn and ask him. "Let's stop for lunch, it'll help you feel better." Leaf was completely knocked out sleeping and didn't hear anything I just said. He wasn't joking I really might need to make the whole trip by myself. I started seeing the other cars were going far beyond the speed limit, so I did the same thing.

We were an hour and a half away from Scarborough, and I saw the car was low on fuel. It was time to get to a gas station and take a break, I pulled into the closest one and tried to wake up Leaf. "Fam, we need to get gas." I told Leaf to wake him up and we woke up in a panic. He starts yelling "Yo fam where are we? Why aren't we at the hotel?" Leaf forgot every single thing that happened this morning, and at this point I had to start laughing. "Fam, we're close to home. We got everything already. We just need to fill up, you need some food cause you were drinking crazy last night, and you got to drive the rest of the way now it's risky. How you feeling?"

Leaf was shocked he let me drive, but he was clearly impressed. He gave me money for gas and food then started stretching. I came back with two burgers, a coconut water, and a Gatorade for Leaf. It was like he came back to life after eating. We filled up the Lexus and were right back on the road. We got back into the city limits and went to the Town Centre parking lot to call Paulie.

"Hey, yes, we got the lasagna with the extra spicy meatballs and sauce with it, how long you going to be? Sounds good, I'll be there soon. No, no problems at all went smooth. It's not about the pasta, it's about the sauce. Haha drive safe." Leaf ended the call and told me what happened, "Yeah, so we got to go to Paulie's house to deliver it, then I am going to drive you right back home. Sounds good?" I replied, "yeah fam, good looking out again on everything, how much is our cut?" Leaf gave me a look like he knew, but he wanted to surprise me with it; "Well, obviously this isn't really thousands of dollars' worth of Lasagna, we got to meet up to get the cash."

We drove to Paulie's house, his Rolls-Royce was parked outside. Paulie has a nice brown, two-floor house with a big driveway. We went to the door with the backpack, and Paulie opened the door before we could ring the bell. We go inside and he has champagne at the dining room table ready with three glasses out, he pours the glasses and asks us to cheers. Paulie raises his glass, we follow his lead and raise ours as well, "Salute, to this promotion and many more!" We tap our glasses together and drink champagne.

When we finished, Paulie took the Santo Marco paper bag out of my backpack and gave me a plastic bag full of cash. Me and Leaf headed back to the Lexus to count it; it was over ten-thousand dollars. "So how much is my cut?" I asked Leaf again. "You did half the driving, so you get half, we do this again in a month, and you have ten thousand to buy yourself a car on your sixteenth birthday. After that, next goal is buying your house and chasing your dream." I thanked Leaf for everything again and he drove me home.

I was so excited, but I knew I had to stay humble and save the money for what Leaf told me. I went upstairs and Natasha and Antoine were out somewhere, so I opened my safe and saw how much money I had saved. I had more than enough for the car I wanted to get. Now I want to map out the rest of my goals. The car is set, music studio is set, I was happy and content with the apartment setup, but I was thinking about starting a college fund. I knew the more money I had saved up meant the more freedom and options I had. If I kept my spending short like I have been, I should be able to make everything work out.

The goal is to start taking music seriously again, get through the rest of the school year, and get my license right on my sixteenth birthday to buy a car. I need to get my passport, too, so I can see Mimi when I need to. I need to make sure that I start going back to church, too. I want to learn how to start investing. There's a lot of things that I have done that I need to start looking to God for forgiveness for, and I need to make sure I don't lose myself to the streets. This year has been a crazy ride that I wasn't expecting at all or ready for, but I am taking none of what is happening for granted.

Chapter Seven:
March Madness

It was another Sunday morning in Downtown Montreal, Quebec, at the same Hotel me and Leaf would stay in what seemed like every weekend for the past three months. There was a sheet of snow covering the mountain in the center of the city which hadn't melted yet, although it was mild at the end of the season. I hadn't even taken the time to count the amount of money I had made through these trips, but I knew it was more than enough that I didn't need to keep doing it. Leaf seemed like he could keep doing this forever if he needed to, but he didn't want to. He was considering changing his car and his license plate, getting paranoid that the police might be catching on to us.

Bottom line is that we still had goals to reach, but we can't reach them from behind bars. Devon was going to be in a basketball tournament over March Break, scouts from universities are going to be there looking to recruit, and I had to be there to support him. Mimi was going to come back to visit family during that time, and I had to finish songs for an EP I started writing. Everything was finally falling back into place. I came an exceptionally long way from where I was in September, but like Leaf said, I didn't come this far just to come this far.

Everything was already loaded in the car, and we were ready to head back on the road to Scarborough. We wanted to get something to eat before we left. There was a homeless man sitting on the sidewalk outside of Santo Marco's, he appeared to look around late fifties, tanned skin, and had on an old and worn Montreal Canadiens beanie with a long black and grey single braid going down his back. He called over me and Leaf, "Hey, I don't want cash, if yous guys are going in there, think you can get me a slice?" Me and Leaf, our nature was to help other people and give back, so Leaf told him "Come inside we'll get you a proper meal."

He goes straight towards the washroom to wash his hands and comes back to meet us by the table Leaf and I were sitting at, and we introduce ourselves. "They call me Leaf, and this is like my little brother, Crisis." Leaf told him. "Name's Alvin, why do they call you guys that?" Leaf responded, "My names Kalief, Leaf's just short form." Alvin then turned to me and asked me, "Are you Native?" I was confused as to why he was asking me that at first, but I responded, "I have some Native roots, but I never felt like I was close enough to that side of the family to claim it. How did you know that?"

Alvin continues, "The name Crisis, who gave you that nickname?" "It was my dad, he went by the name, he wanted me to hold onto it in his honour, and I did because it's the only thing I have left from him." Alvin pauses for five seconds, and asks me another question; "Your dad is Joe Ibanez, right?" I almost jumped out of my seat, but I had to ask, "How did you know my dad?" I didn't think Alvin could blow my mind more than he already did, and then he told me, "Because I'm his uncle, I'm your grandma's brother.

Your dad was a very noble man, and the name Crisis came from being a leader during the Oka Crisis back in the Nineties. Our family has been through a lot, but you have resilience built into your DNA. You have a very bright future if you know how to stay grounded and focused, and you need to be able to. I don't want you to wind up like me or your dad. I hope the next time I see you; you can do more than buy me pasta.

I met you when you were a baby, you wouldn't remember, but you were always the chosen one for me, your dad, and all the elders. He wanted you to make music, and you need to. The world needs to hear your story, and the world needs to have people like us making decisions. I am already where I am in life, you have the time and the resources to make substantial changes in this world. Make sure you use your time wisely to make these things happen." I was stunned listening to Alvin, all I could really do as I was taking in his message was nod and agree. I don't know if he understood I was listening to every word and was just speechless, but I was glad we took the time to talk to him.

You can learn from anybody and everybody in life if you are willing to listen to them. Successful people can tell you what they did to succeed, unsuccessful people can tell you what they would have done differently to succeed, and some people can show you there is a lot more to life other than succeeding. Leaf told me a long time ago that we live on stolen land built by slavery. It was one thing to not honour that system and be a rebel with a cause within that society. It was another thing, and way more important, to fix that system so that the next generations will not need to go through what we did.

We got back to Scarborough and Leaf dropped me outside of my sister's apartment, I had a lot to process and think about on the six-hour road trip and wanted to take it easy for the rest of the night. When I got upstairs and unlocked the door, to my surprise, Natasha, Antoine, and Mimi were all sitting down on the couch watching a movie. "SURPRISE!!!!" Mimi screamed out loud, tapping the couch telling me to sit down next to her. I sit down to give her a hug and a kiss, then keep my right arm around her back and watch the movie with them. "When did you come into town?" I asked her.

"A couple of days ago, where have you been mister?" Mimi asks, as she pulls the strings of my hoodie down. "Not here haha, just got into town, too. Was working in Montreal again."

Natasha rolled her eyes and chimed in before taking a sip of her soft drink, "Yeah, he's in Montreal more than he's here nowadays." Mimi laughed and said, "well, are you staying out of trouble these days?" Natasha's soft drink came out of her nose, and she jumped off the couch laughing. "When you think about it, Crisis never been in trouble before 'cause he never got caught yet."

Mimi stopped Natasha and stood up for me; "that was unnecessary, Daniel knows what he's doing and it's temporary. He's helping the community too and is putting out music, *that* is what he is going to do long term." Natasha understood, swallowed her saliva before responding, and after a tear fell out of her right eye, she told Mimi what she was thinking, "My bad, both of you. Mimi you got to understand though, that is my little brother, all we have is each other. He might have you, I might have Antoine, but Daniel's the only direct family I have left, and I still don't want him to feel like he needs to stay where he is at all."

Mimi and Natasha hugged it out, and then we went back to watching TV. The next day was the first day of March Break. Me and Mimi were going to spend the day at the mall on a double date with Devon and his girlfriend, Desiree. Devon and Desiree have been together since they were in grade nine, she was a grade older than Devon and was graduating this year. They were on-and-off and a lot, and I didn't like the way she treated him. She was always accusing him of cheating, being rude to him and his friends, taking breaks just to be able to see other guys. It made no sense that he was about to be the next Kobe Bryant, and this is who he wants to be his Vanessa. She was using him for a come up in the future.

Today was a big day for Devon and he needed to be focused. Once we got done walking around the mall, Devon had to be on point and ready for the tournament. He had family fly out from all over to see him play, there were scouts from the University of Florida, University of Kentucky, and University of North

Carolina. Devon's dream school was Florida. After spending his whole life in Toronto, the idea of spending a couple of years somewhere warm with beaches was always going to be his first pick. Devon knew one thing for sure, he had to get the offer from them today.

As we were approaching Centennial College, I grabbed Devon's shoulder, and we had a talk. "You ready for this?" I asked him, and he responded, "I am a little nervous about everything of course, fam, but this is what I have been training for my whole life. My family needs me to win this, and I need me to win this. The outcome of this tournament can change the whole future of my family, and this is my destiny. I got to fight through and honour it." I nodded my head and agreed, "You're right, fam, you got this. We been waiting for moments like this since we were in elementary school. I've known you my whole life and I know you're about to achieve something big, just needed to know that you know you're about to." We shook hands, hugged, and then he went into the changing room.

Devon went on to score a total of 30 points in his team's first round, twenty-three points in the second round. In the grand finale, he scored a record-breaking 113 points, winning the tournament. This was the most points ever scored in a Canadian high school basketball game, and the third time a Canadian high school basketball player could surpass one hundred points in a single game. James, the recruiter from Florida, spoke to him before and after the game. They exchanged contact information, and Devon was guaranteed a scholarship as soon as he graduated. His family was extremely proud, and they brought Devon and Desiree to celebrate the good news. I wanted to go, too, but I knew it was getting late and I would need to drop Mimi off at her house.

There was one last thing I wanted to do since we still had a little bit of time left before curfew. I brought her back to our secret spot by the water. Mimi got emotional and told me something I wasn't expecting; "I had a nightmare about us the other night." I felt something choking me inside and was worried about what this might be about, but I had to ask her, "What happened babe?" Mimi explained, "we were in this car, and then the police pulled us over. They arrested you and your friend, Kalief, and left me on the side of the road."

She continued, "I spent the rest of the dream crying wondering where they took you to and was scared that I would never hear from you again. I am trying to be strong for you Daniel, I really am, but this is really starting to take a toll on me. I don't know how much longer you can do what you're doing." I took a minute and asked her, "What are you saying Mimi?" Mimi took a deep breath and then responded, "I'm torn. I never want to leave your side, and I know you would never leave mine. I'm scared everyday somebody is going to take you away from me, and I'm going to be powerless to prevent it from happening." I looked inside myself and I assured Mimi, "Next time you see me, one hundred percent, I'm going to be out of the game, and I'm only going to be focused on music."

Mimi looked me in the eye and said, "How sure are you?" I responded, "One hundred percent, hopefully by the end of the month. Music is really hard without you here." Mimi asked surprised, "Why is that?" "When you were here, it was a feeling of fulfillment, having fans and followers is cool, having people know who I am is cool, but seeing your reaction, knowing you saw how far I could take it, made me want to take it there. You're my muse." Mimi was confused, "But I am still beside you. Send me what you've been working on tonight and let's try that. You can't give up on your dream and you can't try to make excuses for it. I want us to be able to raise our future family one day knowing we overcame everything, and we helped each other reach our dreams, babe."

"You're right." I told her, "I'm going to record as soon as I get home and I'm going to send you the rough copies," I gave her a kiss, and then I walked her back to her house before 9pm.

I got home and started recording songs I've been writing. Before I knew it, I had a full ten song EP ready to edit for release. I sent them to Mimi, and all that was left to do was send the files to someone who could mix and master them, but I knew I was ready to make the comeback to music I've been waiting for. Releasing music after going through trials and tribulations is hard to do, people who have never lived the life of an artist can't fathom or understand what it's like. While you heal and overcome obstacles, you are explaining to people who don't even know you or how you did it, paving the way to be an inspiration for others.

SK King *(7:06pm)*

Yeo Cee, you bless?

Me: *(7:07pm)*

Yes fam, back to music got a project I am almost done, how have you been healing?

SK King: *(7:09pm)*

Yes man, going to be back to full strength soon, your cousin just stopped by to check on me. Was wondering why you have not been checking on him too.

Me: *(7:11pm)*

How? I thought he was in jail I was waiting for his phone calls.

SK King: *(7:12pm)*

They found him innocent on all charges about two weeks ago, he and his mom were trying to get a hold of you. I told him I would tell you to message him.

Me: *(7:13pm)*

Yeah, I appreciate that, I will go hit him up right now.

Me: *(7:15pm)*

Fam, you, okay? It is Daniel I just talked to SK.

Jay Ibanez: *(7:18pm)*

Hey little homie, yes, I am good yo just kicking it. you and Tasha living good from what I heard.

Me: *(7:20pm)*

Yes, we out the hood, I am trying to buy a place for us down south somewhere soon as I can, you gotta come with me.

Jay Ibanez: *(7:22pm)*

Is that why she told my mom you two were not trying to move back? It is good that you are doing good and that you two are going to make it somewhere, but that is not in my future. My life started here, and it is going to end here. You got talent, your sisters got talent, you got a girl that loves you. You all need to go out to fulfill your destinies. My destiny is right where it left off last summer. I don't expect you to understand, but I need you to respect it.

Me: *(7:25pm)*

I had no idea your mom reached out to us. Thought she was still done with me. Either way, I hold nothing against anybody, you are family, and I still want the best for you, and I want to be there for you and Auntie.

Jay Ibanez: *(7:30pm)*

I appreciate that cuz, but what's best for me is to stay right here and look after my mom and look after my hood. It may not be worth it to you, it may not even make sense to you anymore, but it does to me and that's why I do it.

"Hey Natasha! Why didn't you tell me Jay was out?" I shouted from my room asking. "Come in the same room if you need to talk to me." She replied. I walked out of my room to the living room, to see Natasha smoking a joint of cannabis. "Your aunt wanted us to move back in with her sure, and Jay got released from jail, but what would we be going back to Daniel? If we coming with rent money every month you think the landlord is going to get bored and drunk one day and kick us out? You think after months of living here, building up a life where we can be self-sufficient as siblings and stand on our own, you think mom and dad would rather us depend on someone else's housing? We can own our own houses in the next couple of years at the rate we're going, we aren't the same people we were back in August, we're going to abandon all progress just to go back to the square one. For what? So, you can get dragged into a murder investigation? One where they WON'T miraculously lose all the evidence? So, you can have your friend Jason's people driving around waiting to see you in front of the jerk spot? For what, Daniel? For what? I'm seriously asking you Daniel, FOR WHAT?" I tried opening my mouth, but I knew Natasha was right. We overcame too much, went through too much to just go back to where it all started.

The weekend came, and it was time to head back on the road. I took the time to show Leaf the latest music I was making, and we played the rough draft of each song for at least the first hour of the trip. While we were looking for something else to play for the rest of the trip, a fifth wheeler to the right of us starts to lose control, almost knocking us off the road, and scraping the paint of the royal blue Lexus. We pulled over to check ourselves and check the car, there was a clear white scrape from the rear bumper all the way to the front passenger door. Me and Leaf are shaken, but we get back into the car and continue the trip.

About a half an hour later, we get a call from Paulie, "Hey, how's the road life going for yous guys?" Leaf responded, "it's messed up, some trucker just crashed out and scratched up the side of the whip." Paulie laughed it off, "yeah, those guys can't drive worth dick huh? Get that painted over somewhere, you don't need attention on your car till you are back in town." Leaf looked me in the eyes and started talking back to Paulie, "what do you mean get it painted over? That's it?" Paulie started laughing again "obviously that's it, what you thought we were friends? I'm paying you two mooks to do a job, you go to jail you're shit out of luck, on your own, and you owe me money for the shipment. Now grow a pair and get that shit painted over. Go into one of those small towns off the highway now and do it. What you do with the money you been getting for this, huh? Take care of it." Paulie hung up the phone.

Leaf looked over to me and I looked back at him. When I started, he told me this lifestyle wasn't going to last forever. Leaf was already heavily invested in cryptocurrency, and I was heavily invested in music. The guys who survive this business and make it out, are the ones who plan and make a conscious decision and effort to make it out. This accident was a blessing in disguise. Neither of us were hurt, and we both knew exactly what we needed to do once we finished the mission.

We went into the next town, a small town called Napanee. We went to the first car repair place we could find, the owner looked at us, looked at the car, and said, "I can have this as good as new for you for three-hundred dollars, sound good?" Me and Leaf split the cost and waited for it to be done. We went back to get the car and it looked brand new, but the mechanic warned us about not letting the paint dry; "I don't want you guys to get flagged, if you can wait a little bit now, it might just save you a whole lot of time later on." "Thank you for the work but it should be fine." Leaf responded, then we headed back onto the road.

The whole job was so routine to me, it really did feel like it was another day at the office. We go to Santo Marco, pick up the order, and drive back to Toronto. We were about halfway back to Toronto the following morning, when we saw something weird.; There were a bunch of police cars pulling over a royal blue Lexus, the same make and model as Leaf's. We had no choice but to keep driving, but this was a big sign to stay alert, and to be ready for anything. For assurance, we turned on the news channel on the radio to see if anything was mentioned.

"The weather is getting warmer, however, this week it is expected to rain for the first half of the week. Traffic is calm on the 401 Highway going both ways as most people have already returned home from March Break. In sports news, the Toronto Maple Leafs have been able to defeat the Tampa Bay Lightning in order to break their biggest win streak since 2018. However, fans are still curious as to whether or not they will bring the Stanley Cup home this year. When we get back from these advertisements, the Blue Jays are ready to announce their new coach!"

It was just a coincidence, we were reading into a situation that had nothing to do with us, we were overthinking. It wasn't reported yet, either way, we had to get the job done and then we can worry about the rest when it's time to. We made it into the city two hours later. We drove onto Paulies Street, and it was game over. The entire street was blocked off, from the distance we could see the police coming out from Paulie's house, escorting a handcuffed Paulie into a police SUV. As soon as we noticed that we had sped out, we were in the car that they were looking for and they knew what was going on.

We drove for about ten minutes to get away from the scene. Leaf turned to me and told me, "You can't put it in the dumpster, we've been holding it on us this entire time, we need to burn it." I was shocked and didn't believe him. "How? This is so much money we're losing, I- "THEN WE LOSE THE MONEY!" Leaf shouted, "You just saw the buyer get arrested did you not? The same way we need to take losses in the streets, they take losses in the streets, too. If it were flipped, they would have burned ours with no resistance. I told you from the beginning, this wasn't going to last forever, there was going to come a day when we needed to pull out. I can find a new plug, but this package is a dub and I got to sell this car."

I opened the containers inside the paper bag and emptied them onto the bottom of the bag. After, I sprayed the paper bag with body spray then put the lighter to it. We watched it burn, and eventually, it was all ash. There were little particles revealing something was burned there, but nothing that could ever be used as evidence and come back to us. It was sad to see all that money gone, but it was the end of the road.

"Look, take what you have stashed up, we're going to put it into crypto and that is going to be the new trap. We really don't need to do this no more, fam. It was time to let it go. I can make other connections if we really need to go back to this, no problem." Leaf was shaking his head while telling me, knowing deep down he wished it lasted a little longer, but it was time to let it go. We had a wild run in the last ten months, and we made it out without any jail time, anyone dying, and got the future to look forward to. I couldn't help but think what we could have done in twenty months, but there was no point.

My cousin Jay did time in jail, my friend SK almost entirely lost his life. I didn't realize until this moment I had completely normalized gambling with my life. All the time back in the Eastside, all the times I risked my life for survival, it is confusing to figure out if all of it was worth it. I know somebody's prayers were getting me through all of these hardships, but it was time to start praying for myself. It was time to follow purpose instead of survival.

Me: *(8:25pm)*

It's done. I am out of the street life. Not in the gang, not in the trap, clean. You liked the songs I sent you?

Mimi Singh: *(8:27pm)*

Yes!! We are listening to it right now on the way to the airport. I knew you still had it in you. But are you okay babe?

Me: *(8:30pm)*

Everything is fine, just finished the last job, and I wanted to let you know that you don't need to worry about me ending up in any trouble again. Not for a while at least lol.

Mimi Singh: *(8:32pm)*

Thank God, I am really grateful to hear that. You have so many guardian angels watching over you as long as you made it out of that. Even before you moved out, I would be worried about you deep down. You have too much to offer this world to let your environment destroy you.

Me: *(8:35pm)*

Thank you for always having my back and never giving up on me, I wouldn't have been able to do it without you for real.

Mimi Singh: *(8:36pm)*

I wouldn't have been able to handle moving without having you to talk to every day either. I love you Daniel, I am really grateful to have you.

Me: *(8:37pm)*

You always got me, we meant for each other, and I am going to do whatever is in my power to make it work for us. Walking away from the streets was step one. Have a safe flight back home and make sure you call me when you are back home. I love you, Mimi.

Mimi Singh *(8:38pm)*

I love you too, we're going to get through everything together, I'll call you soon as I can.

Tay (Don't Answer): *(9:05pm)*

Hey bro can you let me hold a half gram? I can pay you back next week.

Me: *(9:07pm)*

Man, lose my number you couldn't be associated with me being a drug dealer but you're always bothering me for free drugs. I'm not even selling anymore to anybody but especially not to you.

Tay (Don't Answer): *(9:07pm)*

Why do you Cancers take everything so personally lol let's catch up then what you doing next weekend?

Me: *(9:10pm)*

I'm busy. You should have known I was never going to let you, or Devon get caught up in any problems, but the second things went left you turned on me. I'm never forgetting that, and it is personal.

Tay (Don't Answer): *(9:10pm)*

Look bro I'm not going back and forth with you. Can you spot me or not?

Me: *(9:11pm)*

I'm blocking your number. Hope it was worth it and I wish you the best in your future endeavors.

Chapter Eight:
Unsettled Debt

It's a Tuesday morning in April, it rained last night and the streets are still wet but starting to dry from the morning sun. I walked into Mr. Hadi's class, gave him a handshake, and sat down. I see that he left a flyer on my desk for the school's talent show coming up next week. I ask him, "do you think I should perform?" Mr. Hadi chuckles, and asks me, "Well, do you think you should follow your purpose? What is the point of high school if you're not doing the things you're enthusiastic about?" "Graduating?" I reply.

Mr. Hadi went into philosophic mode, "When you came into my classroom in September, you had a bright future ahead of you, and you still do, but you let something outside of your control dim your vision. There's more to life than money, the same way there's more to high school than graduating. As an adult in your life who cares about you, I can't tell you to do anything, but I think if you don't get back to creating music, there's going to be something way bigger on your lists of regrets when you get to my age."

I couldn't say anything at the moment, but I knew he was right. I went home after school that day and got right to work. I had ideas for songs and deep down, I *did* want to get back to work. I had the house to myself until around midnight, and I was going to make use of it. The first song I recorded was over the same beat Leaf showed me on the way to Montreal back in January. I called it, "*Street Life*." It was always going to be about everything I went through the year prior, leaving the neighborhood, trafficking, still dealing with the same old beef, but I never really sat down and pushed myself to write it.

The second song was on another beat I bought some time ago. Sometimes you can buy a beat and the beat is not right for that time, but can work later on. Every artist has experienced this. It had an old R&B sample from the 1980's or 1990's, and an older styled bassline and drum pattern. I knew I wanted the song to be for Mimi but was insecure about her being all the way in Orlando. The title came to me, "*Distance.*" I got to work and wrote it out.

The third beat was more of a heavy hitting-anthem type of beat. It had a staccato woodwind sound that a lot of trap songs had and a melodic synth under toning the rest of the beat. The 808 was blaring loudly in my headphones but was smooth and consistent. It was going to be called "*Hustle Up,*" this song had to be an anthem for everybody working hard, everybody on any type of hustle, and everybody pushing themselves to get better. I took a little bit longer to write this one because it was a different type of energy. When you're out hustling, you're not exactly focusing on the *why* and *how*. It's more of a bottom line that you need to be productive, so putting it into words took a little bit more than what I initially thought it would.

The fourth beat was a little slowed down and had some indistinguishable samples. For some reason, it made me think about what my long lost relative in Montreal was telling me about Native people. I was thinking about things Mr. Hadi told me about civil rights and the discrimination Black people were also faced with. I was also thinking about what I had to experience here in Scarborough. I decided to call it "*Oh Canada*" and talk about the reality of what happened and continues to happen over here.

There was one more beat I owned, and after writing out four songs, I felt like I was on top of the world. I felt like I was my old self again, the me before getting kicked out, before having my innocence taken away and having to do the evil things I got forced to do. My good side came back in full swing. This song was going to be called, "*I Can't Lose*," and was going to be a song people can listen to when they need to believe in themselves and their power. I got the hook and verses done and went right into recording all of them.

I had a full EP at my disposal by the end of the night. The next step was to send the recording files to a producer who could mix and master them. Once I got the files back, I could upload them to all of the streaming services. I was going to release it independently, the same way I always have, but this would serve as an EP and Demo to send to record labels. I decided to self-title it, *Crisis*. I emailed the files and had to wait a week to receive them back, but I was definitely signing up for that talent show.

The next day of school went great, but as I was walking to the bus stop after school one day, I saw a black Acura TSX with limo tinted windows waiting across the street. It gave me an eerie feeling, like it was the ghost of Jason in a new vessel. I walk to the bus stop and I can feel whoever is in the Acura is staring me down. I sit down on the bench at the stop and hear an engine driving slowly behind me. The car honks, as I turn my head, I realize it's the Acura. The driver lowers the window and puts his hand out of the window signaling me to come over to him.

"What is it?" I shout over, and the driver rolls down the rest of the window. It is an adult Italian male, very obese, with glasses on. "Come over here right now, I ain't joking." He says to me with an entitled tone of voice, "You and your buddy, Kalief, you guys owe us a package, where is it?" I looked him dead in the eyes and told him, "I have no idea who you are, therefore, I can't owe you anything. Have a good evening." He starts chuckling and reveals himself, "I'm Tony. My brother,

Paulie, he sent me to make sure you weren't running off, looks like you are planning on it."

"I don't know Paulie either. I can't help you." I start to walk back to the bus stop when I hear the car door open and feel a push from behind. The push was very weak and didn't do anything other than annoy me. "I SAID I CAN'T HELP YOU!" I shouted at Tony, as I saw him lifting up his sweatsuit, revealing a 9mm handgun. "You have been warned. You better start helping me or it's going to get very messy for you." Tony exclaimed as he walked back into his Acura and sped off. I called Leaf immediately.

"Yo" Leaf answers, "Fam, your boy from the Mafia, his brother or somebody just came and threatened me if we don't pay back what we owe them." Leaf laughs and goes, "Tony? Tony just don't got anything going for himself since Paulie got arrested. He's trying to bully you into giving him re-up money. Paulie owed me a favor for putting him on my team before we met, I gave him an ounce on consignment and the whole thing went right up his nose. Those dudes tried to rat on us, we don't owe them anything. Not now, not ever. Don't worry about none of that."

I took a few seconds to gather my thoughts and then responded; "So this dude is just lying, right? I don't have anything to worry about?" Leaf kissed his teeth and repeated himself. "I just told you Crisis, he is nobody. Never has been nobody and never will be nobody. If Paulie comes out of prison in Five years and needs it, I can take it out of crypto myself. Until then, I am telling you, we are in the clear, and even if that did happen, they tried to snitch on us, did they not?"

"Yeah, you're right," I responded, accompanied by a sigh of relief, "Just got to ask you to be sure, right?" Leaf said, "yes, of course, some people just don't have a purpose. They only exist in this world to leech off of other people's accomplishments and bring other people down to their level. You just can't ever fall for it, little bro. What you saying though for the rest of the night? You want to come over?" "Yeah, for sure, fam. I can be right there." I went to spend the rest of the night at Leaf's crib with him and Lacey.

The day of the talent show arrived, I was excited but nervous. I had my playlist ready, and I just got the e-mail with the final edits from the engineer I knew, Marlon. I would be able to upload them to streaming services once I got home tonight. I went into the gymnasium where the show was taking place, and in the distance, I saw Tony. He was staring me down like he was ready to take my life away today,

I went on to do my first song at the talent show, which was Oh Canada. It was Mr. Hadi's favorite song that I had showed him, and I felt like it deserved to be on the stage for the political message it had. The song received a standing ovation, everybody loved it, and I felt a rush from the positive energy that I had not felt since last summer. I got handshakes and high fives from everybody on my way off the stage and out of the gymnasium.

It was very refreshing and grounding to be back in the zone where I am focused on what matters. I went to the washroom, and while I was at the urinal, I heard somebody else come in behind me. Before I could fully finish, I felt a punch to the side of my cheek. I stopped and instantly zipped up my pants, and turned around to see Tony, angry rushing toward me. He tries to hit me again, I block it, grab him by the collar of his T-Shirt, and punch him straight in the face, breaking his glasses before running out of the washroom.

I get back to the gymnasium and sit down, acting like nothing happened. I get a tap on the shoulder from Ms. Caruso to go with her to the office. I go there and see Tony sitting down, and I sit down beside him, and Ms. Caruso starts talking, "So, this gentleman right here, Tony, graduated from this school just before you started grade nine. He's here as an alumni guest to watch the talent show, do you recognize him?" I told Ms. Caruso exactly the truth. "Miss, he came inside the washroom and punched me while I was peeing." I had no loyalty to him and no reason to get in any type of trouble with this guy, so I didn't care at all.

Ms. Caruso nods her head, "So I am going to review the cameras outside of the boys washroom, if it is true that he came into the washroom after you, we will ban Tony from returning to this school. In the meantime, you know that Pope has a zero-tolerance policy for violence, and we need to send you home. You are suspended for three days until this is all settled." This got me instantly heated, "Miss, look at the tapes right now and it's going to show you the truth." "I hear you Daniel, but I need to have the other staff present to make the decision, this is serious." I get out of my chair and leave the school.

Leaf calls as I'm stepping out the front doors, "Yo, Crisis! How did the comeback show go?!" "Yo, I'm killing Tony tonight. Man came here and attacked me in the washroom, now I'm suspended. I am waiting right by the bus stop to see his car and where it goes. Get over here we're going to need to follow him--" Leaf stops me, "Fam, go home. I told you; the man is trying to make you crash out and trick you into throwing your life away. Don't fall for it. He's a nobody.

It's not worth it. Snipa was worth it. Shotty was worth it. Go home. We just got out of the game, why do you want to go to jail now for? You just got back to taking music seriously, why now? You got so much going for you right now that this man is jealous of, he's trying to take away from you. This man is doing this to you for a reason, if you do anything to this man I promise you, he will call the police on you. You're not related to him and nobody around him will think differently of him. Go home."

After battling with my demons for about half an hour, I took Leafs advice, and went home. I wasn't happy about it. It was the hardest thing I ever had to do, to let a man disrespect me like that and just walk away. There were too many things going on for me that if I let myself crash out over this it could destroy everything. I got into my sisters apartment, put everything away and just spent the rest of the night on my phone.

Every choice in life is either a step forward or a step backward. I could have waited and stabbed Tony, God knows how badly I wanted to. God also knows how badly I want to make things work with a girl in another country, how badly I want to be successful in music, and how badly I want to be able to do good in life. Killing somebody or damaging somebody else, whether they deserve it or not, can take away the potential to do all of those things. He might have one up on me here, but what I am willing to work for in life. Someone like Tony would never be able to understand or fathom what I can achieve in life.

Me: *(1:00pm)*

I am home. I didn't do it.

Leaf Wade: *(1:11pm)*

You made the right call fam. You don't have to prove anything to anyone anymore. All you have got to do now is be the voice these kids in Scarborough and kids around the world need. Everybody is willing to do twenty-five to life over something that will not even matter two months into the future. Focus on music, which is the new trap, show them that the only thing from that street lifestyle worth doing is chasing money and getting out of that lifestyle. You can't do that from a jail cell.

Mimi Singh: *(2:30pm)*

Hey! Saw the footage from the talent show on my friends feed, I am so proud of you for keeping up with challenging work babe. You overcame so much in the past year, and I am always on your team no matter what happens I am always rooting for you. I love you.

Me:*(2:32pm)*

I love you too Mimi, you always got the number one spot no matter what to me. I'm so grateful I got you in my life you have no idea. Everywhere I go in life I got to make sure I'm bringing you along with me.

Chapter Nine:
Sweet Sixteen

Hello Crisis,

I listened to your new album, everybody here did, and it is incredible! You have a natural ear for music and know how to make hit after hit after hit! I always believed in your potential and saw the natural raw talent. America needs enthusiastic artists that are as polished as you. You are a talented individual with a gift for personally connecting with listeners. The team here at Digital Records has unanimously decided we would like to re-visit our previous offer, are you available for a call tomorrow at 11:00AM EST? I will send a Zoom link in a separate e-mail for you to accept.

Best Regards,

Michael Williams, (position)

Digital Records

Mike,

Absolutely not, zero percent chance. If you listened to the new album, then you know what the emergency was. You know what it was I was going through, you and your "team" have already proven to me that you all are not going to have my back when push comes to shove. You showed me no remorse, understanding, or patience, you showed me that I am nothing but a potential paycheck. I mean no disrespect at all, but I deserve better than that. I don't care how it comes across. If I am as good as you tell me I am, I can wait for another offer.

Blessings,

Daniel "Crisis" Ibanez

I was really about business; I always answered my emails first thing in the morning. The thing is, Digital Records wasn't the only label sending me e-mails now, and I test each of them. I tell them all now is the wrong time just to see how they react. The ones that understand, those are the ones that *might* get a call back. In the meantime, I'm making enough money on my own as an independent artist. Enough that I won't ever need to sell a gram of anything again. If I ever want to live in a place like the Eastside again, it will only be to give back to the community and because it is the right decision.

I had just finished my exams and got straight A's in every single class this year. I'm right beside Devon on the Honour Roll. He did everything he could to ensure his full ride scholarship ever since he met the scout from Florida. Mr. Hadi convinced him to study kinesiology, then he'd have back-up options; Physiotherapist, league coach, anything that would keep him where his heart is.

Natasha was the one waking up early for school now. She's attending beauty college to get her cosmetology license. Antoine's attending barber school at the same time. They both had the same dream and were planning to open a barbershop and beauty salon together. He proposed to her on Mother's Day last month, and they're planning a private wedding. I really didn't like him at first, just saw him as someone who thought he was too good for certain stuff. After living with him for a year, I've realized everybody is too good for certain things, we just need to wake up and realize it.

Jay and SK are the same as they've always been, still E.S.C. until the end. Some people can be happy with what is comfortable to them, even if it's not the best lifepath, you need to respect their decisions and choices. It doesn't matter if they make different decisions than you would. Jay has always had my family, and S.K. has always had my family, and that love will always remain. I just got to hope nothing else bad happens to them and they choose better when they see me do better.

The first thing I had to do for the day was go check Leaf, he wanted to get into music management. I would be his first artist. I didn't have anyone else that could trust to hire, and if I couldn't trust Leaf after the year we just survived together, I couldn't trust anybody. I get to his apartment, knock on the door, and he opens up and gives me a dap and a hug. "Yo, Crise, I gotta show you something first before we even talk about business." "Yeah? What's up with you?" Leaf goes into the washroom and runs back out, holding a pregnancy test.

"What are you telling me right now, fam? You and Lacey ready for that step?" I asked him and he smiled in a way I had never seen before, ear to ear, and he responded, "Yeah of course, bro. We got the crib, we got the cars, we out the trap. There's no reason not to start." I was happy for Leaf, but I worried. I respect him and I want to be supportive, so I collected my thoughts and made sure I answered and came across in that light, "You're really that sure we're never going back to the trap?"

Leaf laughed and responded, "That's what the second thing I got to show you is." Leaf goes into his phone, and makes a phone call, putting the call on speakerphone. "Hey, Leaf Wade?" the voice sounded like your average middle aged White businessman. Leaf responded, "Yessir, I'm with the artist I told you I'm managing, Young Crisis, I want you to tell him exactly what it is you told me."

111

"Hi, is this Young Crisis? My name is William Acter, I work for the City of Toronto. We want you to perform at our upcoming Canada Day celebration. We will be paying you five-thousand dollars cash, and it will be an big opportunity for you to perform in front of a large audience and be on national television. What do you say?" I was stunned. Streaming money was enough to get by with, but to make that much in one day really affirmed that I was on my way. I instantly replied, "You have my full commitment Mr. Acter. I will be there."

William continued, "Thank you, how old are you by the way? We need to be sure that if you are under the age of sixteen that you will be – "Leaf interjected; "He is going to be Sixteen in two weeks, right before the show. Also, you promised if he does a respectable job, it will lead to further opportunities and the showcase afterwards can pay upward to ten-thousand dollars, correct?" William paused, and responded, "Correct." Leaf gives me the look one more time and ends the call, "Thank you so much for your time, William, you will be happy with this decision. Have a wonderful day." "You two as well. Happy early birthday, Crisis."

Leaf gives me a hard dap and yells, "I TOLD YOU I WAS GOING TO BRING YOU HERE!" I was mind blown, "Yeah you did, you really been the truth since day one." "Everything happens for a reason, Crisis, you got to always remember that. If we didn't meet when we did, and where we did. We would both still be down bad. I knew you trusted me with a lot of different things, and I had to honour that. I wasn't off rip expecting to do all this that first day in the shelter, but I knew giving you the opportunity was the right call."

Leaf continued, "We're going out to celebrate! I know you aren't crazy about partying, but we turning up today!" I nodded my head and agreed, and we got into his car. As we approached it in the parking lot, Leaf handed me his keys and walked towards the passenger seat. "You can use some practice," Leaf told me. "I didn't get my license yet though, need two weeks." Leaf busted out laughing and lightly punched me in the shoulder. "All the shit we had in this car, and you worried about something *now*?!"

I laughed it off and unlocked the car with the fob button, "yeah, good point." I told Leaf, then I had to ask; "So where are we heading?" Leaf told me. "Caviar Cadence, downtown. I am going to text SK and Jay to come through, too. You ever try smoking shisha?" while shaking my head no, I told him, "Not really, they have that there?" Leaf was ecstatic; "Yes. Yes, they do. You are trying something new tonight boy."

We arrive at the restaurant, a valet in a white dress shirt and burgundy vest greets us and parks our car. We walked inside the restaurant, and right at the front were Jay and SK We all give each other daps and wait for our table to be ready. After about five minutes, a waiter came to the front. "Do you gentlemen know what you would like to order or would you need some time with the menu?" SK went first; "Fried Calamari and Nachos to start off, maybe garlic bread too."

The waiter nodded, "That can be arranged, do you know what you would like for your main course? "For the main course for me, steak and lobster pasta." SK concluded. Jay ordered next, "2 pounds of suicide hot wings for me please." Then Leaf, "risotto al caviar, and let me get a Caesar salad to go with it." The waiter looked at me and before asking, I got the same choice at a new restaurant. "I'll just have a veggie burger with fries please." The waiter responded, "As you wish, what will we be drinking?" We all said "Water," and he took away our menus.

He came back with a jug of water, and we all raised our glasses. "Salud to better money and bigger opportunities." Leaf shouted, as we touched our glasses, Jay shouted, "Happy birthday little homie!" SK instantly gave Jay a back-handed slap across the chest, making Jay spit out his water. I paused confused and asked, "What's going on guys?"

Leaf gave both SK and Jay a look and put his index finger across his lips, "How the hell did y'all go twenty plus years of life without snitching?" Leaf said while shaking his head. Leaf shrugged and told us, "Aii fine, so there's a surprise birthday party for you. Your girlfriend and sister planned it. We just came here so they could set up your apartment for when we dropped you home." I looked at Leaf in shock, "She's here right now?" Leaf kissed his teeth and said, "Yes, man, obviously." I had more questions, "How would you drop me home, weren't you guys coming upstairs too?" Leaf looked at me again, "No, we would wait for five minutes, then come up."

"I don't really know what to say." I told them, "Thanks, man. I appreciate it, but yeah, I'll act surprised." We tapped our glasses again and then the food came. We ate and left without trying shisha. We drove back to Scarborough and got to my building, I could see Mimi on the balcony, but she didn't see me since we're still in the car.

I get out of the car, head into the lobby, and go upstairs. As I'm putting my key in the door, I can hear Mimi and Natasha mumbling to each other. "He's here just get it ready!" I heard Natasha say under her breath. I opened the door, and I saw everybody; Mimi, Devon, Tay, Lacey, Natasha, Desiree, and Antoine. "Happy birthday," they all screamed at the top of their lungs; with a huge blue banner across the living room wall, surrounded by blue balloons everywhere.

Hip Hop music was playing, there was a big chocolate cake, and it had a picture of me as a kid printed on it with two candles, one in the shape of a one and another in the shape of a six. I blew out my candles and Mimi ran up to me right after to give me a hug. "Thank you for everything, babe." I told her and gave her a kiss. Tay came up to me and felt this was the right time to talk to me, "I'm sorry man, I should not have been like that with you. I was being selfish, we don't need to be close like we used to be, but I want you to know that I have thought about how I was, and I wouldn't do it again." I gave Tay a dap and a hug. "Thanks for apologizing, man, I really appreciate it. We're cool, don't worry about it." We nodded to each other and I went to talk to Mimi.

I went outside and I pulled Mimi close, I gave her a huge kiss, then we looked out into the sunset, and I finally asked her, "You had so many options in Orlando, what made you decide to wait on me?" Mimi looked deep into my eyes, chuckled, and answered, "The same reason you had so many options in the club, and decided to wait on me." *Real love is releasable; if two souls are meant to find each other, they will, and no matter how far apart they may seem, they will always reconnect in the end.* I am one hundred percent confident that I will be marrying Mimi if she lets me, and I would never have it any other way. We are still young, and I couldn't ask for more, but I know more is coming.

If you have a girl like Mimi right now reading this, you got to keep her. If you have a friend like Devon, you need to stay loyal to him and keep him close. If you have a friend like Leaf, you don't need to involve yourself in everything Leaf does, and if he is a real friend, he will not want you to anyway. The point that I am making is, if there is any lesson to take away from this book, more than anything else it is that the people around you will either build or destroy you.

You don't need too many people around you, but if you have the right people closest to you, you can reach your maximum potential. If you have the wrong people around you, they can rob you of everything you have ever wanted. No matter what life throws at you, the solutions are simple, and you need people who are going to make life and keep life as simple as possible for you. If I had to be in constant chaos with everybody around me, I wouldn't have been able to get anywhere through the course of this book. Remember that.

To be continued...

To be continued.

www.ingramcontent.com/pod-product-compliance
Lightning Source LLC
LaVergne TN
LVHW091225080426
835509LV00009B/1165